**Church, State and Schools
in Britain, 1800-1970**

Church, State
and Schools in Britain,
1800-1970

James Murphy
Senior Lecturer in Education
University of Liverpool

London
Routledge & Kegan Paul

First published 1971
by Routledge and Kegan Paul Ltd
Broadway House, 68-74 Carter Lane, E.C.4
Printed in Great Britain by
Northumberland Press Limited
Gateshead
© James Murphy 1971

ISBN 0 7100 6950 2
Set in Linotype 10/11 pt. Pilgrim

THE STUDENTS LIBRARY OF EDUCATION has been designed to meet the needs of students of Education at Colleges of Education and at University Institutes and Departments. It will also be valuable for practising teachers and educationists. The series takes full account of the latest developments in teacher-training and of new methods and approaches in education. Separate volumes will provide authoritative and up-to-date accounts of the topics within the major fields of sociology, philosophy and history of education, educational psychology and method. Care has been taken that specialist topics are treated lucidly and usefully for the non-specialist reader. Altogether, the Students Library of Education will provide a comprehensive introduction and guide to anyone concerned with the study of education, and with educational theory and practice.

J. W. Tibble

Church, State and Schools in Britain, 1800 to 1970, in the history section of the series, sets out to unravel the complicated history of the religious question in British education. In his *The Religious Problem in English Education: the Crucial Experiment* (1959), the author has already published a fascinating case study on this issue, but one concentrating specifically on the situation in one city – Liverpool – in the mid-nineteenth century. Here he goes fully into the background of the key Acts of Parliament which established the 'dual' system – of Church and Local Authority (or Council) schools. Particular attention is devoted to the formative period before the 1870 Education Act, and, of course, to that of 1902 which for the first time allowed Church schools to be financed out of the rates. The changing policies of different religious groupings are analysed, and their outcome in legislation brought out.

If the religious issue is no longer as important a feature of educational debate as it used to be, nevertheless the battles of the past must be understood before the complex forces which have moulded the existing educational system can be fully realized. In addition, many of the problems fought over in the past are still with us, and await resolution. Dr Murphy's book is a scholarly and authoritative study of this question, and will be of value to students and others who wish to understand its relevance and complexity.

Brian Simon

For
A.-B.M.

Contents

Acknowledgments   xi

Introduction   xiii

Abbreviations used in the text   xv

1 The forces at work   1

   The state and the Established Church   1
   Churches, schools and political alignments   4
   Attitudes of teachers and parents   6

2 ' "United education" is an impossibility'   10

   State provision for the education of the poor   10
   The changing status of the Established Church   12
   The 'religious problem'   13
   The 'Irish System'   15
   The first government grant, 1833   16
   The political parties and the Established Church   17
   The 'Irish System' and the 1839 government plan   17
   The Committee of Council on Education   21
   *The 'rights' of the Established Church and the
      Factory Bill, 1843*   22

3 'Progress by administration'   26

   *Kay-Shuttleworth and the Committee of Council on
      Education*   26
   The 'Concordat' of 1840   27
   The Tractarians   30
   The Voluntaryists   30
   The 'management clauses'   32
   The Minutes of 1846   34
   The grants to Wesleyans, Roman Catholics and others   35

The single-school area and the 'conscience clause'   37
Problems of expense and administration   41
The deficiency in educational provision   40
Local aid and control   42
Attempts at legislation   43

4   The Elementary Education Act, 1870   49

The League and the Union   49
'Filling in the gaps'   51
Financial provisions of the Act   53
The problem of religious instruction   56
Reactions of Denominationalists and their opponents   60
Some results of the Act   62
The position in Ireland and in Scotland   64

5   The Act in operation   65

The school boards   65
The 'new type of Pope in the Council Office'   66
The boards and the Cowper-Temple clause   67
Progress towards agreement   70
The alignment for future conflict   73

6   The Education Act, 1902   76

The political situation after 1886   76
Rate aid for denominational schools   78
Denominational instruction in board schools   80
The new local authorities   81
Preliminary skirmishes in parliament   82
New attitudes towards education and welfare   83
The administrative 'muddle'   84
The proposed 'way out'   85
The Anglican proposals   87
The contribution of aided voluntary schools and training
     colleges   88
Joseph Chamberlain and the Nonconformists   89
The Bill in parliament   90
Chief provisions of the Act   92
The conscientious objectors   94

7   Attempts to modify the 'settlement' of 1902   96

The Liberal Bills of 1906-8   96
Decline of active secularism in the Labour and Socialist
     movements   100

The failure of the Fisher proposals of 1920   101
The 'Scottish solution' of 1918   102
Denominational schools and 'secondary education for all'   104

8   The Education Act, 1944   110

The climate of opinion   110
The need for action   111
The policies available   112
The rival interests   113
Provisions for religious instruction   115
The reactions of the churches   118
The concessions of 1959   119

9   The end of 'passionate intensity'?   121

Changing attitudes in the Free Churches   121
The teachers   122
The Education Act, 1967   123
*Denominational and public authorities and modern
     education*   124
New views on old policies   126

Select bibliography   130

Books for further reading   142

Index   144

Acknowledgments

I should like to record my sincere gratitude to Professor Brian Simon for his very helpful comments and his generous patience as editor, and to Mr John Vaughan, tutor-librarian of the School of Education at the University of Liverpool, for his professional efficiency and friendly concern to procure not only the works I sought but others newly come from the press, apparently known only to him, and, I shall always suspect, written at his instigation in an increasingly desperate endeavour to make me well-informed.

J.M.

Introduction

The simple terms 'church' and 'state' obviously stand for complex realities. Sometimes the first may refer only to the clergy; at others to the great mass of believers, including or excluding these; sometimes, in effect, to those churchmen influential in political life, whether clergy or laymen. When one speaks, for example, of the financial contributions made by this or that church for the erection and support of schools, one needs to remember that more than clerical support was usually involved (though in fact many of the clergy made great sacrifices of time and money); when there is talk of church control of education, one needs to know precisely whose control is meant; and one must not be surprised when sincere supporters of a church vote in parliament for measures deeply resented by its clergy. The writer hopes, without great confidence, that, where confusion might arise (and he is not himself in doubt), he has always made the position clear. Again, it would be wrong to think of the state as consisting only of the governments and the parties which produced them. In Britain governments, as we shall see, are often glad to allow the permanent and experienced administrative officers to persist with, or even to initiate, arrangements which it would be highly inconvenient to have debated; and incoming governments are quite commonly relieved when civil servants demonstrate to them the difficulty of changing policies inaugurated by their opponents and therefore recently denounced in the heat of party strife.

It would be extremely wrong to think of the state as continually straining to establish an admirable system of education, but being thwarted by the churches. It is true that the disputes between the churches weakened the influence of those who strove to set up a national system of education, and delayed its establishment by presenting apparently insoluble problems; but the enthusiasm for popular education among political leaders throughout the period was not remarkable. Many reasons, from economic theories to the cost of wars, were in all periods advanced to restrain or restrict action; the prime ministers (Gladstone and Balfour) connected with two of the three major Education Acts were astonished and appalled at their eventual cost.

Since what follows is largely a history of conflict one can hardly expect the parties engaged to appear at their best, and it may be necessary, in justice, to point out that many of those who, in effect, did most to hinder the establishment of a national system of elementary education (Lord Ashley and the Rev. G. A. Denison are examples) were very generous in their support of schools for the poor.

Further, this is not a study of church and state angrily disputing for the right to foist divergent views upon the people. In the earlier part of the century, indeed, fears of the political theorists that the state might use the schools for its own ends appeared a little unreal in the face of its very moderate interest in elementary education and its reluctance to assume greater responsibility than was required to ensure value for money. There was even some apprehension lest schooling might lead to disaffection. When the state committed itself to the support of elementary education almost all thinking men of both of the major political parties would readily have echoed the routine declaration of the first secretary to the first government committee concerned with education, that it was 'essential that the Government should avoid every form of interference which could discourage individual enterprise [and] the freedom of opinion' (Kay-Shuttleworth, 1853, 292). But two observations need to be made. The first is that it was taken for granted that both church and state were in duty bound to inculcate, as undoubted facts, social, economic (and sometimes religious) views which many now would regard as highly debatable justifications of the existing order. The second is that the state could rely with complete assurance on the willingness of almost all who conducted schools to encourage the political attitude which mattered most of all – one which the Rev. John Keble so lucidly described as 'a cheerful submission to authority, a desire to find one's superiors in the right'.

Lastly it is well to note, as the author has tried to do, that much that has happened in schools, especially since 1870, has had little to do with what church or state intended – more with what school boards, managers, teachers, sometimes parents, and occasionally even children, were prepared to give, or to take.

Abbreviations used in the text

(Extended titles are given in the Bibliography.)

C.C.   Cross Commission
M.C.C. *Minutes of the Committee of Council*
N.C.   Newcastle Commission
N.S.R. *Annual Reports* of the National Society
R.B.E. *Reports of the Board of Education*
R.C.C. *Reports of the Committee of Council*
R.S.P.C. *Return ... schools for the poorer classes ...*, 1870
R.R.T. *Returns ... respecting the religious teaching ...*, 1888
T.E.S. *The Times Educational Supplement*

I

The forces at work

The state and the Established Church

When the state assumed supreme control of the Anglican church in the sixteenth century it became imperative that both should work together, not least because whoever sought to change the national religion might well seek to change also the organization of the state (and *vice versa*), so that heterodoxy in religion might be allied to disloyalty or treason in politics. Thus, quite apart from the importance attached to religious instruction as an essential part of education, it seemed logical that schools and universities should be prevented from producing potential enemies of both church and state, and that the government should decree that the licensing of teachers and the provision and oversight of education should be under 'the control and auspices' of 'the established Church of the Realm'.

In the early decades of the nineteenth century the 'special relationship' between the state and the Established Church remained extremely close. The head of the state was the head of that church; bishops were nominated by the state, often to reward or to ensure political support; changes in the church's liturgy and laws were controlled by parliament; its prelates sat in the House of Lords. Not only were most church appointments at the disposal of the Crown or of the ruling class, who could appoint congenial clergymen to them, but the prevailing admiration in the highest church circles for 'rational' religion, the scorn felt for 'enthusiasm' and 'visionary' fervour, made it easy for leading Anglican clergymen to move socially among influential laymen not remarkable for their piety; and, indeed, for numbers of such laymen, or their nominees, to become Anglican ministers, especially since 'England was probably the sole country in Christendom where no proof of theological knowledge was exacted from candidates for ordination' (Halévy, 1949, I, 391-2).

It was widely agreed that the church must hold a privileged posi-

1

tion in the state. The Anglican parish priest remained legally the pastor of all those living within his parish. Nonconformists, equally with Anglicans, could be obliged to pay tithes (often to lay patrons of benefices) and to contribute towards any church-rate levied for the repair of the nave of the parish church and the upkeep of the churchyard. No one (apart from Quakers and Jews) could be legally married except by an Anglican clergyman, and where, as usually was the case, the only graveyard available was that attached to the parish church, Nonconformists were buried according to Anglican rites or with none at all. No one could be awarded a degree at Cambridge, or even be admitted to Oxford, without subscribing to the Thirty-nine Articles of the Church of England, and all senior members of the universities had to conform to the liturgy of the church.

But serious disadvantages for the church flowed from its close association with the state. Among politicians easy social familiarity with the clergy often bred, if not contempt, at least a certain genial irreverence, and a disposition to suspect that demands made in the name of the church were inspired by a desire for perquisites or influence. In other ways the sources of the church's strength were also sources of weakness; as when, later in the century, the state delayed the establishment of necessary new bishoprics so as to prevent any increase in the church's representation in the Lords; or when needed reforms were opposed by churchmen who felt obliged to deny the state's right to effect them, or else were rejected by legislators anxious to protect their interests and patronage. Much criticism was aroused by nepotism, the wealth enjoyed by many clergymen (although others were desperately poor), non-residence and sinecures; and there was bitter resentment that many of the clergy were led by political and social sympathies to become agents and allies of unpopular administrations, to be 'ministers of the government rather than ministers of the gospel', as one contemporary critic complained (quoted Bowen, 1968, 5).

Moreover, by the beginning of the nineteenth century the need for an alliance between church and state, in the field of education or elsewhere, had much diminished. Society had become much more secular in outlook. The Industrial Revolution and the requirements of commerce and science were creating a need for studies far beyond the purview of most of the clergy: and if the traditional public schools and grammar schools had become outdated in the eyes of many middle-class parents, they offered still less to the illiterate poor. The growth and movement of population were making the church's parochial organization and geographical distribution inadequate. Again, experience had shown that differences in religious belief, though still capable of arousing considerable suspicion and hostility in many quarters, need no longer lead to disaffection and civil strife.

The state was confronted not with one church but with several, for most Scotsmen were Presbyterians, most Irishmen Roman Catholics; in England and Wales Nonconformity had been greatly strengthened by the rise of Methodism, and there were considerable numbers of Baptists and Congregationalists, with influential groups of Quakers, Unitarians and Presbyterians. It has been claimed that in 1811, 'while the nominal members of the Establishment still constituted an enormous majority, the Nonconformists already equalled, if they did not exceed, the Anglicans who practised their religion' (Halévy, 1949, I, 428). The laws prohibiting Protestant Dissenters from teaching had been repealed in 1779, and had fallen into disuse earlier. Similar freedom had been extended to Roman Catholics in 1778 and 1791. Moreover the Evangelical revival which had strengthened and revitalized Nonconformity had led to the development of an Evangelical group within the Anglican church, remarkable for its piety, philanthropy and devotion to the Protestant religion – and therefore able to work readily with Nonconformists. The first Evangelical bishop was not appointed until 1815, but by that time the influence of the group was considerable, and it was destined to increase.

But in the meantime the lack of religious zeal and the admiration for 'practical Christianity' to be found among leading Anglicans made it the easier for 'reasons of state' to prevail. Thus, in the hope of increasing political stability in Ireland, parliament in 1795 established a seminary to train Irish Roman Catholic priests at Maynooth, the same grant being made annually for maintenance; in 1799 the government even planned to pay both the Presbyterian and Roman Catholic clergy in Ireland, ten of the Roman Catholic prelates agreeing, in return, that no one of whom the state disapproved would be appointed a bishop, none who had not taken an oath of allegiance a parish priest. The proposals were dropped only when Roman Catholics were refused entry to the Westminster parliament following the Act of Union (1800).

In 1807 parliament debated, and the Lords rejected, Samuel Whitbread's proposal that local rates might be levied in England and Wales by vestries or magistrates to provide elementary education for poor children. The Archbishop of Canterbury complained that the Bill, if passed, would 'subvert the first principles of education in this country', since education should be 'under the control and auspices' of the Church of England; but one speaker, Earl Stanhope, opposed what he called 'the abominable principle that no part of the population of this country ought to receive education unless in the tenets of the established church'. He asked a question which

3

was ignored at the time but which would eventually have to be answered:

> Was it reasonable or just to say that the children of catholics, presbyterians, quakers, and all the innumerable sects of dissenters from the established church in this country, were to be barred all sources of public education, supplied by public benevolence, unless they were to become converts to our established religion? (*Hansard*, IX, 1177).

Churches, schools and political alignments

Whatever the reply might be, there was still very general agreement that the education of the poor should be provided by the churches and be primarily concerned with religious instruction. From the 1780s the Sunday schools spread rapidly. At first some efforts were made (as in London, Birmingham, Manchester, Liverpool, Stockport and elsewhere) to provide Sunday schools on a non-sectarian basis, but the desire of the religious bodies to teach their particular doctrines, or to guard against proselytism by others, proved too strong almost everywhere. Relatively few schools taught more than religion and reading, it being frequently objected that writing and arithmetic were servile pursuits unsuited to the Sabbath. But the development of the cheap monitorial system by the Quaker Joseph Lancaster and the Anglican Andrew Bell during the early years of the nineteenth century made it possible for the churches to establish considerable numbers of day schools providing instruction in religion but also in the three R's.

Nonconformists in the larger towns established many schools in which their own particular beliefs were taught, but many others supported the schools assisted by the British and Foreign School Society (founded, in its embryonic form, in 1808), the aim of which was to promote 'the Education of the Labouring and Manufacturing Classes of Society of every Religious Persuasion'. It was one of the Society's original rules that 'the lessons for reading shall consist of extracts from the Holy Scriptures; no catechism or peculiar religious tenets shall be taught in the schools, but every child shall be enjoined to attend regularly the place of worship to which its parents belong'. In view of claims made later regarding the Society's success in providing an acceptable form of 'non-sectarian education', two facts should be noted:

(*a*)   The rules did not forbid explanation of the Scripture extracts read: in 1838 the secretary of the Society informed a 'Select Committee on the Education of the Poorer Classes' that children were interrogated and explanations given in accordance with 'the plain and obvious meaning of the text'. Whilst proselytism was forbidden, he admitted it to be 'very possible that in all cases, to a great extent, the opinions of the master will colour any explana- tions of the master, however simple those explanations may be'. The Society received for training as teachers every year 'probably equal proportions from the Church of England, Wesleyans, Con- gregationalists and Baptists', and 'no practical difficulty' arose except that 'a small proportion' of the Unitarians objected (Qq. 524, 508);

(b)   the official historian of the Society has recorded that 'from the beginning there was no attempt to conceal the evangelical tendency of the instruction given. Doctrines like those of the Trinity and Atonement were plainly taught; though the main causes of offence, as between the various sects, were carefully avoided' (Binns, 1908, 113).

The Church of England set up in 1811 a rival association with the significant title 'The National Society for Promoting the Educa- tion of the Poor in the Principles of the Church of England'. Again, not all Anglican schools were affiliated to the Society, and, of those which were, by no means all were assisted by it. In the schools in union with the National Society (as it came briefly to be called) definite rules were laid down which became important in later con- flicts: the teachers must be Anglicans, though children of all sects were admitted; all pupils must not only read the Authorized Ver- sion of the Bible but be taught the church liturgy and catechism; and all must attend an Anglican church on Sundays.

The provision of schools for Roman Catholic children was particularly inadequate because of the relatively small numbers of middle-class subscribers and the constant influx of miserably poor immigrants from Ireland: thus in Liverpool in 1824, though the ratio of Roman Catholics to others was probably about one to four, the proportion of children in Roman Catholic schools was less than one-fifteenth (Murphy, 1966 (2), 114). The children were forbidden by their priests to attend schools (even such as those of the British Society) where the reading of the Authorized Version was insisted upon, though they were permitted to attend for secu- lar instruction where no attempt was made to influence belief, as in some Unitarian and other schools (ibid., 114 n.).

It must be emphasized that the division of opinion about school provision was not always rigid. Children of different persuasions were often to be found in one school. Many Anglicans and others of different denominations, and of none, supported the schools of the British Society. Clergymen and others of all creeds sometimes established schools out of sheer kindness towards poor children, not troubling about doctrinal differences. But, generally speaking, such differences were considered highly important among the clergy and their more committed followers, including many politicians – though some of these were, of course, ready to exploit prevailing prejudices. Moreover, even when the immediate cause of dispute was a policy regarding schools, the antagonism often arose from a deep underlying hostility not primarily dependent on educational or even theological opinions. Among the clergy the contest often took on that special degree of bitterness to be found when members of a profession criticize each other's ministrations as inadequate, heretical and positively harmful, and therefore deny to each other recognition as qualified practitioners, or even socially acceptable colleagues. An Anglican clergyman would often consider his dissenting colleague brash, 'dismal and illiberal', and he could hardly have been expected to relish criticism of his own religious beliefs as lukewarm, Erastian and a betrayal of the principles of the Reformation. The dissenting minister, often debarred from performing burial and marriage rites; seeing the followers on whom he depended for financial support obliged to pay rates to a wealthy 'state' church and send their children to Anglican schools and churches; and finding himself despised by Anglican pastors for the very lack of university education which church and state denied him, could perhaps be understood if he angrily opposed policies which to him seemed designed to make use of schools to strengthen the position of the Established Church.

The committee of the National Society included, among others, all the Anglican prelates, and it naturally represented those most anxious to propagate Anglican doctrine : it became all the more important a guardian of the church's interests because it was sometimes regarded as the only substitute for the church's constitutional governing body – Convocation – which had not met since 1717 (Denison, L.E., 1902, 40). It naturally looked for support to the Tories. Though in general the Nonconformists sought help from the Whigs, many Wesleyans still looked upon themselves as faithful members of the Church of England, and it has been observed that 'at the beginning of the Victorian era the dominant political tradition among the Methodists was Christian Toryism' (Vidler, 1949, 115). The British and Foreign Society was supported politically and financially by many Whigs, and also by many Radicals, Socialists and others anxious to change the social order and to attack the power and pretensions of the Anglican Church : so that political antagonism and religious hostility were very frequently merged.

Attitudes of teachers and parents

Until 1870, at any rate, the opinions of teachers in the schools for the poor carried little weight. The two education societies from the first made arrangements to give rudimentary training to their own teachers: but Roman Catholic teachers were sometimes trained in Anglican establishments (Southey, 1844, III, 448), and, as we have seen, Anglican teachers were admitted to the training institutions and schools of the British Society. Some teachers set up professional organizations open to all denominations, though in 1823 Dr Bell showed disapproval of such associations (ibid., 293). In general the qualifications, pay and status of teachers were so low that independent expressions of opinion could hardly be expected of them: they might at once be dismissed for any infraction of rules relating to religious instruction, or even at the whim of a new incumbent. When Samuel Wilderspin, already widely known for his influential advocacy of infant schooling, ventured to contradict an Anglican clergyman in 1837, he was contemptuously informed that the latter could not 'consent ... that a clergyman of the Church of England should stand to compete with a schoolmaster' (Murphy, 1959, 116).

More remarkable were the attitudes of the parents. For most of the period covered by this book religious and political passions raged fiercely among many clergymen, politicians and their warmest supporters about the kind and degree of religious instruction to be given to the children of the poor; yet, broadly speaking, one can say that at the centre of this storm there was a great calm area occupied by the vast majority of the parents of the children concerned. (And we are not here discussing the mass of the desperately poor and brutalized inhabitants of the worst slums, who for most of the nineteenth century were scarcely touched at all by religion or by schooling.) It is true that working-class Roman Catholics tended to follow loyally the instructions of their priests, partly because of the more strict demands made on them by their religion, the greater sense of unity engendered by their position as a small minority and their close association with their clergy. But the Church of England had failed to develop in the quickly expanding towns the influence it had long possessed in rural areas: as one Anglican clergyman remarked in 1896, 'It is not that the Church of God has lost the large towns: it has never had them' (quoted Inglis, 1963, 3). Again, except in a few areas of England and in parts of Wales, as the nineteenth century went on, Nonconformity tended to become associated more and more with the lower middle classes and those just above them in the social scale, especially since prudent and thrifty workers (whether attracted to religion by being so or made so by their religious beliefs) naturally rose out of their class. In 1902 Charles Booth, writing on the *Life and Labour of the People in London*, found that

'The great section of the population which passes by the name of the working classes ... remains, as a whole, outside of all the religious bodies. The bulk of the regular wage-earning class still remain untouched, except that their children attend Sunday School'.

Not that most parents were unbelievers, in spite of the efforts of Radicals and Socialists to spread secularist views. It has been said that at the beginning of Victoria's reign

> ... most slum pastors agreed that the poor were free or almost free of infidelity. They found apathy and indifference and hostility, not unbelief.... The literature of the working man was violently anticlerical, antichurch, antimethodist, antichapel. It rollicked in abuse of the establishment. But it was not usually heathen. Pamphlets and newspapers used simple texts of scripture to beat church of merchant and chapel of shopkeeper. Most working men would have been horrified to be told that they were not Christians (Chadwick, 1966, I, 333).

It was widely accepted that, rightly given and received, a modicum of religious instruction would improve character and conduct. One experienced observer reported in 1859: 'Even those who themselves have very little religious thought of any kind, have a notion that religion is a good thing for their children'; another declared:

> The religious element ... I found, was considered essential, and that element consists in reading the Bible. The mass of the poor have no notion as to any distinction beyond that between Roman Catholics and Protestants.... I am satisfied that the working people would insist upon having their children taught the text of the Bible, but that they are willing to permit any man professing Protestant opinions to explain it (N.C., III, 528, 66-7).

But although there was often some resentment of compulsory attendance at Anglican churches on Sundays, and some feeling (not by any means universal) among Protestants against their children attending Roman Catholic schools and *vice versa*, the evidence is overwhelming that most parents who sent their children to school, especially in the towns, were far more concerned about the quality of the education than about the religious doctrines taught. As the Rev. W. F. Hook, the influential Anglican Vicar of Leeds, wrote to Gladstone in 1843, by far the great majority of working-class parents would say 'give a good secular education, cheap or gratis, and you may, as pay, inculcate your own religious doctrines' (Stephens, 1881, 347). Sometimes it was felt that erroneous doctrines could easily be countered at home; sometimes that the precise difference between one branch of Protestantism and another was hardly likely to be grasped by a child attending school for a year or two and leaving at the age of ten or eleven; more often there was indifference. But only extensive quotation, not here possible, could demonstrate how frequently throughout the period here covered qualified observers reported that in England itself 'the religious problem' was of little practical concern to parents who were not Roman Catholics or Jews – and often not to them.

Faced with masses of such evidence from its Assistant Commissioners, the Newcastle Commission (1861) pointed out that, whatever importance parents might attach to secular education, the 'leading object' of the founders and supporters of the schools was 'the improvement of the poorer classes in a moral, and, above all, in a religious point of view'. It agreed that 'the comparatively passive attitude of the body of the people' might 'materially diminish' the practical difficulty of introducing a generally acceptable system of religious education; but it pointed out, unanswerably, that 'it was not with the body of the people, but with the founders and supporters of schools, that those who might attempt to introduce it ... would have to deal' (N.C., I, 39).

2

'"United education" is an impossibility'

State provision for the education of the poor

The cheapness of the monitorial system made possible the widespread establishment of elementary schools in the first decades of
the nineteenth century: moreover children were almost always
expected to pay fees, and, even at 1d. per week, these usually provided no inconsiderable part of the expenditure. But the cheapness
depended on the availability of at least one really large classroom,
and the report of a Select Committee on 'the Education of the
Lower Orders in the Metropolis' (1818) recognized the need for
state grants in aid of building, since, as Henry Brougham informed
the Commons, plans to establish schools were often abandoned
'because of the first and greatest expense' – that of 'providing a
school room and a master's house' (*Hansard*, XXXIII, 587).

It was not the general climate of informed opinion which prevented the state from complying with the recommendation for
the next fifteen years. In 1805 Bell had proposed 'a scheme of
Education patronized by Church and State, originating in the
Government, and superintended by a member of the Establishment'
(Southey, 1844, 1, 50). In 1814 the British and Foreign Society, in
its turn, had asked for assistance from the Crown (Binns, 1908, 82).
Respect for the doctrine of *laissez faire* was tempered by the fact
that Adam Smith himself, together with such different thinkers as
Priestley, Paine, Bentham, Malthus and James Mill, had emphasized
the importance for the state of the education of the people; they
were followed in this by Robert Owen, John Stuart Mill, and the
curiously influential phrenologists George Combe and James Simpson. True, most of these had warned against complete state control
of education, and many Nonconformists held that education, like
religion (with which it should be intimately connected), was no
concern of governments; but most thinking people were coming

to accept that state aid for education was desirable and necessary, that voluntary contributions and parental payments should nevertheless be required, and that, though full state control would be highly undesirable, some degree of inspection to ensure the proper expenditure of public money would be needed.

As fears inspired by the French Revolution died away, less was heard of the argument that instruction would lead to disaffection, more of the contention that since the state could punish for crime, it could also provide instruction to prevent it. By an odd twist it even became common to advocate state aid for elementary education in order that future workers, having learned that the iron laws of economics made state intervention on their behalf quite purposeless, would not riot or join unions to demand it.

Hitherto the state had rarely concerned itself with financial support for education in England and Wales, apart from the endowment in the sixteenth century of some grammar schools and university colleges (usually from resources confiscated from the church), and abortive plans drawn up during the Civil War and Interregnum. But in Ireland since the Reformation the state had at times made use of educational provision as an instrument of policy, mainly as a means of 'anglicizing', converting to Protestantism, and thereby pacifying, an unruly population: the educational results had been meagre. The Westminster parliament's grant to Maynooth College, already referred to, was clearly politically motivated. But from 1816 parliament made available to the Kildare Place Society fairly considerable funds for the education of the Irish poor (the Bible to be read without note or comment), and displayed real concern to dispel educational destitution.

Shortly before Scotland's union with Britain (1702) her parliament had reinforced earlier legislation by ordering the provision of a school in every parish not possessing one, to be supported by the local landowners and tenants, and with a schoolmaster approved of by the minister of the Church of Scotland. The law was not everywhere observed, and did not apply to the towns, but development was encouraged when in 1803 the Westminster parliament prescribed an increase in the salaries of teachers, who were to be appointed by the ministers and landowners, but must be satisfactory on religious grounds to the presbytery; the ministers would superintend the work of the school. The earlier close connection between these schools and the Church of Scotland was thus perpetuated, and it was strengthened when the Church not only encouraged local congregations to provide schools in urban districts but, through its General Assembly, financed a considerable number of schools (Knox, 1953, 24). In Scotland, therefore, solutions had early been found to some of the problems which were to prove so intractable in England: the provision of money, the arrangements for local control and the relationship between church and school. The last of these presented little difficulty in Scotland since the religious minorities were so small: indeed from 1829 the General Assembly of the Church of Scotland permitted the children of Roman Catholics to attend its schools, 'without taking part in the religious exercises of which their parents might disapprove' (*M.C.C.*, 1847-8, I, lxi).

In England, however, parliament had hitherto taken little interest in the education of the 'independent poor'. True, the first Factory Act (1802) had provided that apprentices in a small number of mills and factories should be instructed in the three R's and given religious instruction (under the supervision of a magistrate and a clergyman); but the expense was to be borne by the manufacturers, and, in any case, the Act was not enforced.

The changing status of the Established Church

One obstacle in the way of state aid for education in the first decades of the nineteenth century was the easy assumption that, thanks to the monitorial system, adequate progress was already being made through voluntary effort; but another was the special status of the Established Church. What powers and rights, in modern times, did 'establishment' confer? In 1818 the state granted one million pounds from the taxes for the building of Anglican churches, with a further half million six years later. In 1823 the government agreed to advise the king to issue a letter asking for 'a General Collection in all Churches and Chapels throughout England and Wales' in aid of the National Society. Further Royal Letters were requested and granted at intervals during the next thirty years (Burgess, 1958, 212). In 1827 the Liverpool Corporation, at the invitation of a Church of England minister, built two schools in which the only religion taught was Anglican (Murphy, 1959, 4-6). In 1820 when Brougham proposed in the Commons the establishment of a system of parochial schools (the buildings to be paid for by manufacturers, the running costs out of low fees and local rates), he felt obliged to recognize what he had earlier called 'the just prejudices' of the Established Church by providing that the secular curriculum of each school would be decided by the local Anglican clergyman, whose approval of the schoolmaster, also to be an Anglican, would be essential. Though the religious instruction would be confined to Bible teaching, where parents so desired the catechism and liturgy of the church would be taught on Sunday evenings. The Church of England leaders rejected this recognition of its special status as trivial and inadequate, but the

Nonconformists and Roman Catholics were now strong enough to denounce it as intolerable.

For theoretical positions were yielding to political realities. In 1828, on the motion of the Whig Lord John Russell, a Tory government under Wellington repealed the Test and Corporation Acts, which now only nominally oppressed the Nonconformists. In the following year the same government 'ran away from its principles', as one die-hard put it, by sanctioning Catholic emancipation (largely because of disturbances in Ireland). Since the Bill was supported by Sir Robert Peel, who had been elected for Oxford University as a convinced and reliable opponent of Roman Catholicism, and since the measure split the Tory party, it can be seen that the tide of events was irresistible. The opposition of almost all of the Anglican bishops to the Reform Bill made them intensely unpopular, and the passing of the Act in 1832 strengthened the representation in the Commons of the Nonconformists in the larger towns, and also of the Roman Catholics (mainly through their co-religionists from Ireland).

Clearly the constitutional position of the church was in danger: Sir Robert Inglis had claimed in parliament that the repeal of the Test and Corporation Acts had 'severed the Church of England from the state', whilst Catholic emancipation would 'sever Protestantism from the state' (quoted Best, 1956, 169). Tory and Whig leaders were far from sharing this view, but it was a natural consequence of the new situation that the latter were pressed by many of their supporters and Radical allies not to allow the traditional claims of the Established Church to prevent the creation of a national, state-aided system of education for poor children of all denominations.

The 'religious problem'

But the demands of the Church of England were far from constituting the only hindrance to state support for education; they must be considered quite apart from the other constituents of the 'religious problem', which at this period may be summarized thus:

(1) The state might have agreed to support everywhere separate schools for each of the different denominations (and perhaps for the various sub-divisions of these).

But, quite apart from the desirability of making the education of children a cohesive rather than a divisive force, there were many single-school areas, that is, districts in which the number of children could justify the establishment of only one school: this was particularly true of rural areas, where the village Anglican school could often cater easily for all available children, and there might be only a few children of Nonconformists. Yet how could the religious instruction of different denominations be provided in one school?

(2) The obvious solution appeared to be the division of secular from religious instruction, allowing the latter, if deemed necessary, to be given separately to children of the various denominations – within or outside the regulation school hours, on or off the school premises, by their clergy, their normal school teachers or others. This policy was advocated not only by many who had no religious beliefs but by many also who thought it the only practicable one, and by some Nonconformists who saw in it a way to accept state aid without condoning state provision of religious instruction.

The Roman Catholic clergy, though they naturally preferred to have their own schools, were at this time prepared to accept this arrangement, but most committed Anglicans and many Nonconformists (especially Wesleyans) insisted that to separate secular and religious teaching was to act upon, and convey to the child, a wholly wrong idea of the purpose of both: a religious atmosphere should infuse all that was done in the school.

(3) Given that religious instruction must be an integral part of the school day, perhaps some form of it acceptable to all denominations could be found?

But the leaders of some denominations denied this, claiming that undenominational religious teaching would outrage conscientious beliefs and lead to apathy, cynicism and irreligion: though the British Society favoured unsectarian teaching, it had to be admitted that an 'agreed syllabus' was difficult to arrive at unless the views of Unitarians were ignored. Moreover there could be no agreement even as to the version of the Bible to be employed. One of the immutable features of Roman Catholic policy was its refusal to sanction the reading of the Authorized Version; yet for a convinced Protestant to accept this implied criticism of the accuracy of his Bible, by acknowledging as equal some version likely to have been tampered with by priests in order to keep their followers ignorant of the truth, was to proclaim himself opposed to what he regarded as one of the great achievements of the Reformation.

(4) There could be a combination of undenominational religious instruction for 'united' classes (so as to prevent segregation either of pupils or of religious and secular education), with denominational instruction given to the separate groups at other times.

This, of course, would meet some of the objections made against other proposals but fail to satisfy those who considered agreed undenominational teaching impossible to achieve and/or harmful.

Thus stated, the 'religious problem' was clearly insoluble.

The 'Irish System'

Yet in 1831 an acceptable policy seemed to have emerged in Ireland. The state-subsidized Kildare Place Society had not won the confidence of the Roman Catholic clergy, who disapproved of its Bible reading without comment, often evaded its regulations and accused it of proselytism. Edward Stanley (later Lord Stanley and, eventually, as Lord Derby, Prime Minister) found when he became the Whigs' Chief Secretary for Ireland that, although 'five-sixths of the population were Roman Catholics, nearly two-thirds of the whole benefit of the Society went to Protestant Ulster; while the other three Catholic provinces had only one-third to their share' (*Hansard*, VI, 1253). The grant was therefore withdrawn, but, largely as the result of the efforts of Thomas Wyse, an Irish Roman Catholic M.P., a Board of Commissioners of National Education was set up to establish in Ireland, with the aid of government grants, a national system of education. The Board comprised seven men: the Protestant and Roman Catholic Archbishops of Dublin, a member of the Presbyterian Synod of Ulster, the Lord Lieutenant and three other laymen, one of whom was a Unitarian. It was decided that, in the schools assisted by the Board, children of all persuasions would receive secular education together, whilst separate denominational instruction could be given, on school premises if desired, at any time on at least one weekday set apart for the purpose, and also on every other weekday before or after 'the ordinary school business'. (By special arrangement, it was agreed later, any preferred version of the Bible might even be read during ordinary school hours, if no child was compelled to be present against the wishes of its parents.) To disarm those who objected to thus separating religious and secular education, and in the hope of removing the barrier of animosity which divided Roman Catholics and Protestants, the commissioners even agreed on specially translated selections from the Bible, to be read by children of all denominations together during the normal school hours. The use of these 'Irish Scripture Lessons' was quite optional, formed no essential part of the 'Irish System', as it came to be called, and was not a condition for receiving state support.

It was astonishing to many that an agreed policy had even been put forward, and naturally the opposition to it in Ireland and England was for a time very great. There was often unmeasured abuse and gross misrepresentation. The most common claim was that the Bible had been 'excluded' from the schools, in favour of 'mutilated versions', at the behest of 'Popish priests': in vain the Protestant Archbishop of Dublin challenged the Lords to say how many of their children, or of themselves, read the Bible so frequently as the children in the Board's schools. But there was support from some of the clergy of the Church of England – and even, curiously, from 'the Lord Mayor, Aldermen and Common Council of the City of London' (*Hansard*, XII, 541). Within a few years the policy had become fairly generally accepted in Ireland, whilst most English critics had lost heart. Although the Tories had bitterly opposed the Liberal policy, they agreed to continue it when they came briefly to power in 1834-5; and when Stanley joined the Tory party the future of the 'Irish System' seemed to be assured. It appeared reasonable to hope that England and Wales would also soon have state provision for elementary education.

The first government grant, 1833

In 1833, J. A. Roebuck, a leader of the Radicals (now allies of the Whigs), put before the Commons detailed Benthamite proposals based on the thesis that there should be 'universal and national' education of the people, to achieve which the 'aid and care of the State' were absolutely necessary. He pointed to the examples set by Prussia, France and the state of New York, and he asked for compulsory education from seven to fourteen; there would be a wide range of schools and other educational establishments, including training colleges, with very liberal curricula, to be administered locally by elected committees. A cabinet minister would supervise the system and the funds would come from taxes, existing charitable endowments and school pence. All denominations would be treated alike. There was overwhelming opposition from both political parties and much fear expressed of state regulation and the discouragement of private charity; but subsequently a poorly attended House voted, avowedly as an experiment, the first annual state grant in aid of public elementary education in England and Wales – the very small sum of £20,000. From the following year, 1834, a grant of £10,000 was made annually for elementary education in Scotland. The state was moving very cautiously. Not only was the sum made available about one-twentieth of the annual education grant of the Prussian government (Adams, 1882, 88), but assistance would be given only towards the cost of building, and at least half of this must come from private contributions. State supervision was limited to requiring the auditing of accounts and the submission by school managers of 'such periodical Reports respecting the state of their Schools and the number of scholars educated, as may be called for' (*Treasury Minute*, 30 August 1833). The 'religious problem' was to some extent evaded by the requirement that in England and Wales all applications for aid must be supported by the National and British Societies, which meant that not only Roman Catholic but also denominational Nonconformist schools, such as those of the Wesleyans, could not receive assist-ance. Because of this, because of the greater resources available to the Church of England, and perhaps also because of greater efforts made, by 1839 about 80 per cent of the state grant went to Anglican schools. Nevertheless two important principles had been estab-lished: the state had acknowledged some obligation to provide for the education of the poor, and it had agreed to devote public funds to some schools not associated with the Established Church.

The political parties and the Established Church

The pressure on the leaders of the Church of England to surrender some of its privileges came from both political parties and was considerable without being overwhelming. In 1833 the Whigs sup-pressed a number of Protestant bishoprics in Ireland and reorganized the revenues of the Irish church, though a motion to devote part of the income thus made available to secular purposes, including education, had to be withdrawn. In 1836 a Whig government provided for the commutation of tithes and made it possible for marriages to be legally solemnized in non-Anglican churches; both of these reforms had been promised by the Conservatives in 1835 (*Hansard*, XXVI, 66). In 1835, also, the Conservatives set up, and the Liberals continued, an Ecclesiastical Commission to recom-mend necessary reforms of the Established Church.

But it soon became obvious that, whilst the more forward-looking Anglican leaders, such as Bishop Blomfield of London and many Evangelicals, were willing to welcome the Commission and accept some reforms, attacks on the status of the church would be strongly resisted, and indeed that neither of the political parties had any intention of proposing disestablishment. Melbourne had roundly attacked in 1834 those Dissenters who showed 'bitter hostility and ulterior designs against the Established Church' (quoted Halévy, 1950, III, 178), and in the same year attempts to revise the laws regarding church-rates and Nonconformist burials were defeated. So also were efforts to make available to Nonconformists the Universities of Oxford and Cambridge. Moreover the Tractarian movement was soon to quicken the spiritual lives of many in the church, and in particular to convince many clergymen of the high importance of their calling: for too long the church had been the handmaid of the state and now, it was believed, the position must be reversed.

The 'Irish System' and the 1839 government plan

As year followed year after 1832 those who had expected the

passing of the Reform Bill to herald a new advance in educational provision became more pressing and impatient. Men like Brougham, Roebuck, Wyse and Simpson constantly put forward proposals; statistical societies reported on educational deficiences in Britain; the Central Society of Education pointed out that 'the great defect of English education ... is the want of a national organisation.... It forms the one great exception to the civilised world' (*First Publication*, I, 161). Comparisons were constantly made with the state of affairs abroad. The British and Foreign Society had declared that popular education must no longer be concerned with the rudiments and should take into account the ideas of Pestalozzi: it proposed in 1838 the establishment of a national system of education 'based on the Scriptures, but ... excluding the formularies of any particular church', and with rights of withdrawal from Bible reading for Roman Catholic and Jewish children. Wyse advocated in 1838 a board similar to the Irish Board of Commissioners in Ireland. But in the same year a select committee of the Commons (which included W. E. Gladstone, a 'rising hope of the Tories'), reported that, though it had found a vast amount of educational destitution and ignorance of religion among the poor, it could only recommend an increase in the government grant and could not even agree that this should be extended to schools in which Roman Catholic children read the Bible in other than the Authorized Version. It is not surprising that Richard Cobden, after trying to persuade clergymen of different denominations to compromise, decided that he would find it easier to campaign for the repeal of the Corn Laws (Murphy, 1959, 41); or that Lord John Russell, as Home Secretary, should inform the Commons that, though he was 'fully convinced that it was the duty of Parliament, and of the state to further and encourage education in this Country', a board of education could not be set up until greater agreement prevailed 'among those who were in favour of general education in this country' (*Hansard*, XLIII, 731-2).

Yet by this time, as we have seen, a national system appeared to be well on its way in Ireland. Moreover in Liverpool the Liberals had introduced the 'Irish System' into the two 'Corporation Schools' in 1836. Almost all the Anglican clergy in the town had refused to co-operate, the leader of those opposed to the policy being the Rev. H. McNeile, an Evangelical Anglican clergyman from Ulster, who, with the Rev. H. Stowell of Manchester and other Evangelicals, helped to found branches of the Protestant Association in many parts of England, 'to agitate', as McNeile himself put it, 'against Popery'. He raised once again the cry that 'the Bible was excluded from the schools' (meaning, as he explained when confronted with the facts, that some of the children read a translation other than the Authorized Version). The local Conservatives welcomed his support and there was much popular commotion at election times; but from the first the Roman Catholic clergy approved the new régime, and, as the truth became known, children of all persuasions began to attend the schools. After two years McNeile acknowledged defeat.

Thereupon the Liverpool Liberals, who had deliberately embarked upon the experiment as 'a feeler of the pulse of England', pointedly called upon Russell, whom they had accused of timid procrastination, to follow their example. He visited the schools, praised what he saw, examined the working of the 'Irish System' in Ireland, and decided, in spite of Melbourne's warnings, to take action. In February 1839 he told the Commons that 'great success had attended the experiment in Ireland', and that greater success still might have been anticipated in England. But consultations with representatives of the Church of England had convinced him that 'any one united plan of education' would not be acceptable to them (*Hansard*, XLV, 287). Nevertheless he announced the government's decision to establish 'under the direction of the state', a training college for teachers with a model school attached. Students and children of all denominations would be admitted, and religious instruction would be both 'special' (i.e. denominational) and 'general' (i.e. undenominational). The denominational instruction would be given at set times by the appropriate clergymen, and the Bible would be read daily, the Roman Catholics being free to have their own version. But, so that religious education would not be divorced from secular, but 'be combined with the whole matter of instruction and regulate the entire system of discipline' (a policy which Russell personally considered important), undenominational instruction would be given to those of all denominations together, as part of the normal curriculum. The only concession made to the Established Church was that the (salaried) chaplain of the institution would be an Anglican clergyman, though he was not, of course, to interfere with the denominational instruction of members of other communions (*M.C.C.*, 11 April 1839).

Russell clearly appreciated that a widespread adoption of the 'Irish System' would be impossible in England without the co-operation of large numbers of Anglican (and other) clergy, but he was prepared to set up one state institution employing the system and try to ride out the inevitable storm until the new policy found reasonably general acceptance, as had happened in Ireland and in Liverpool. No doubt he hoped for the support of most Nonconformists, the Roman Catholics, some of the Anglican clergy and perhaps even of most influential Tories, since, as we have seen, both political parties had now expressed approval of the policy adopted in Ireland.

But the volume and tone of the criticism, even vituperation and misrepresentation, which greeted Russell's proposals were quite astounding: whatever allowances are made for honest misunderstanding and strong emotions it is impossible not to agree with him that there was 'a perverse anxiety to exclude the public from forming a correct notion of the plan' (*Hansard*, XLVII, 1380). *The Times* had praised the Irish System eight years earlier, but since then its editor had changed his political allegiance, and it now called for public meetings to be held in every town and city to protest against this 'anti-national, anti-protestant measure': it spoke of the 'mischief' which would result from allowing the children of Protestants 'to herd with the leprous brood of Papists, Socinians, Freethinkers and fanatics' (18 May, 3 June 1839). Stanley, who had similarly changed sides, denounced the proposals with a fervour undiminished by any thought of his earlier advocacy. Lord Ashley (the future Earl Shaftesbury), claimed that Russell's modest plan was 'hostile to the Constitution, the Church, and to revealed religion itself'. The Protestant Association raised the cry of 'No Popery' and organized protest meetings and petitions in many towns. The government was accused of favouring scepticism, latitudinarianism, secularism and unscriptural education. Almost all of the higher clergy of the Established Church (though not the Bishop of Norwich) were opposed. Even more discouraging to the government was the official denunciation by the Wesleyans, who felt that the plan would 'open a door for the introduction of Popish and other heretical teachers in the pay of the State' (quoted Mathews, 1949, 133). By July 1839, according to the Bishop of London, only 100 petitions had been presented to parliament in favour of the government plan, whereas 3,000 had been against.

Many Nonconformists spoke and petitioned in support of the government, and Richard Cobden helped to organize in Manchester a petition, 'signed in the short space of a week by upwards of twenty-one thousand persons', which asserted 'as an indispensable principle of justice, that all schools supported by the public funds should be, without an infringement of the rights of conscience, open to all denominations of Her Majesty's subjects' (*The Manchester Guardian*, 12 June 1839). But the favour shown to the Church of England by the provision for the appointment of an Anglican chaplain was resented by numbers of Nonconformists as being what the Marquis of Lansdowne privately admitted it to be – a 'sop to the church' (MS. letter, James Simpson to George Combe, 13 April 1839).

The government was in no position to wait for the wildest charges and most exaggerated claims to be proved false: the

Liberals were in power only on sufferance (as the result of the Bedchamber Question), and this, of course, increased the intensity of the political feeling against them. Within two months (i.e. in June 1839) Russell's tentative first move towards a state-provided system of education had failed: the plan to set up a training college was postponed 'until greater concurrence of opinion is found to prevail', and the earmarked grant of £10,000 (first voted in 1835) was divided equally between the National and British Societies. The failure seemed complete, and Brougham wrote: 'We are completely defeated, and defeated without any hope of a favourable reverse of fortune another time' (1839, 17-18).

The Committee of Council on Education

But the triumph of the Established Church and the Conservatives was by no means complete. Although, as Russell said, the government had agreed 'to throw one of our children to the wolf' (1875, 374), it held to its decision to take the distribution of the annual grant for education out of the hands of the Treasury and to set up a special Committee of the Privy Council (usually referred to as the Committee of Council on Education) 'to superintend the application of any sums voted by parliament for the purpose of promoting Education'. Such a council could be appointed by Order in Council, making legislation unnecessary, and it was in this curious way that the state set up its first embryonic 'board of education'. When given an opportunity to discuss the matter, the Commons in fact expressed approval of the creation of the Committee of Council by a majority of only two, whilst the Lords voted overwhelmingly to present an address to the Queen protesting, *inter alia*, against the 'important functions' committed by Order in Council to the Committee of Council without the consent of parliament. The Archbishop of Canterbury, who presented the address, received no encouraging answer.

Russell had not lacked advice as to the possible constitution of a board of education. The British Society had proposed a board which would 'enjoy the confidence of the various denominations'; Wyse, a body of commissioners to include clergymen of the different persuasions together with some laymen, as in Ireland. Disraeli and Gladstone opposed state interference with education; Peel and many other Tories considered it essential that the clergy should be represented on any board of education if, indeed, education were to be taken out of the control of the churches. Brougham in 1837 had proposed a board which comprised two members of the government with three others who, being 'irremovable' and able to outvote the ministers, would prevent the state from exercis-

21

ing complete control over the educational system: he felt that 'there was nothing which prevented a prelate from being one of the commissioners, but ... they would be raising the question, whether a dissenting clergyman ought to be there also'. It was hardly necessary for the Marquis of Lansdowne to comment that 'that was the difficulty' (*Hansard*, XLIX, 330-1). It would clearly have been impossible to persuade representative church leaders to sit together as equals on such a board.

The government made the very important decisions that the members of the Committee of Council should all be laymen, not chosen to represent the churches, and that they would be members of the government, including the Home Secretary and the Chancellor of the Exchequer, with the Lord President of the Council at their head. The membership would therefore change as governments came and went, but there would be a permanent non-political secretary to act as chief administrator. The powers and policies of this Committee will be considered in the next chapter.

The 'rights' of the Established Church and the Factory Bill, 1843

As remarkable as, and still more significant than, the government's determination to set up the Committee of Council had been its confident, almost scornful, rejection of the demand that, in any national system of education provided by the state, the religious instruction should be exclusively in the hands of the Established Church. This claim was still quite often made. Lord Ashley declared that 'The State adopted the Church of England as the true Church, and if it did not enforce her tenets in education it had no right to countenance others' (*Hansard*, XLVIII, 279). The Archbishop of Canterbury presided at a great meeting of the friends and supporters of the National Society at which it was resolved unanimously 'that religious instruction was an essential part of the education of the people at large', and that 'such instruction should be under the superintendence of the clergy and in conformity with the doctrines of the church of this realm, as the recognised teacher of religion' (*The Times*, 29 May 1839). Gladstone had maintained in his book *The State in its Relations with the Church* (1838) that 'the state had a conscience' and that an important part of its duty was to propagate religious truth and discourage religious error: it must therefore support only the doctrines of the Established Church and should not, for example, pay Roman Catholic chaplains in the army or provide the grant to Maynooth.

But, as Gladstone said when an old man, his book 'was written in total disregard, or rather ignorance, of the conditions under which alone political action was possible in matters of religion' (Morley, 1903, 179); though it was by no means true, as he also claimed, that he was 'the last man on a sinking ship'. Peel dismissed his notions simply as 'trash' (Chadwick, 1966, 478), and Macaulay had no difficulty in showing how impractical such views were for a government at the centre of an empire whose peoples professed so many religions – the state had no more need or power to decide what was true or false in matters of religion than a joint stock bank (1839). In the Lords, only two months after the meeting referred to above, the Archbishop of Canterbury declared that the church 'had never advanced any pretention to control all the education of the country', and he 'appealed in confirmation of his statement to the conduct of the clergy in general'. He could not say, however, 'that injudicious language might not have been occasionally used upon this subject' (*Hansard*, XLVIII, 1235, 1251). The Bishop of London had seriously proposed in 1836 that the state should tax coal to provide funds for building Anglican churches in London (Chadwick, 1966, 131); but now, though he claimed that the Established Church was, 'by the constitution of the country, the established and recognised organ of religious education and ought to have sufficient means for the discharge of her functions', he was reluctantly prepared to have the state support the schools of 'dissidents' if this were done 'by way of charity ... not as a matter of right', or at least not in such a way 'as to make it appear that the Government withholds its confidence from the Church' (*Hansard*, XLVIII, 1306).

Nevertheless, for political realists to accept the legal rights of others was one thing: after all, many committed Anglicans, including many of the clergy, had supported the passing of the laws on which these rights were now based. But to accept equality was quite another matter, and the Bishop of London had declared it to be the duty of the Anglican clergy to oppose any measure designed to 'raise all Dissenting sects to a level with' the Established Church; for

> if a system of national religious education were to be based on the principle of giving to the members of every different sect the same advantages as were enjoyed by those in connection with the Established Church, then the Established Church might as well, so far as the connection with the State and the use and object of that connection was concerned, at once abdicate its functions (*Hansard*, XLVII, 759, 757).

The great political influence of the church had just been demonstrated, and even Russell had vaguely promised 'a temperate attention' to its 'fair claims'; whilst Brougham was convinced that 'the alternative of refusing all National Education' was 'to allow some preference, some interference, to the Church' (Brougham, 1839, 17-18). The question remained – what 'preference' could and should an established church be granted?

The Conservatives who came to power in 1841 attempted to answer the question. Peel, the Prime Minister, disliked state intervention in religious affairs but reluctantly allowed Sir James Graham to make an indirect approach to the problem. The state had extended the Factory Laws in 1833 by making education compulsory for children under thirteen in certain factories: there would be instruction for two hours daily and inspectors to ensure compliance. Graham proposed to include in his Factory Bill of 1843 clauses relating to the provision of education for children in workhouses and in cotton, wool, silk and flax factories – hardly a comprehensive measure, but again 'a feeler of the pulse of England'. The state would make loans for the establishment of schools, and maintenance costs would come from the local poor rate. The majority of managers of each school would almost always be Anglicans, including the Church of England clergyman and two churchwardens: the schoolmaster would also be an Anglican approved by the bishop, and there would be weekday instruction in Anglican doctrines, though withdrawal on grounds of conscience would be permitted. Not surprisingly, Nonconformists objected to these plans, whereupon Graham made considerable concessions, among others that licensed dissenting ministers might give denominational instruction once a week, and that four of the trustees might be elected by local ratepayers. But the vehemence of the opposition even to the modified proposals was remarkable, for the Nonconformists felt that their beliefs were to be assailed in the very areas – the manufacturing districts – where they felt most strong, and no concessions could now do much to lessen the anger and suspicion which the original proposals had aroused. Though the Factory Act of 1843, as eventually passed, required parents and employers to see that the children in many factories attended school for half the working week, no regulations concerning religious instruction were made.

Meanwhile the future of the national system in Ireland had been jeopardized by a campaign waged against it by Archbishop McHale of Tuam, who resented any limitation on his freedom to teach Roman Catholic children and gained the support of a number of his fellow prelates. An appeal to Rome for arbitration in 1839 resulted in the issue in 1841 of a papal rescript giving no formal ruling but leaving the decision to individual bishops, and asking the 'Bishops and other Ecclesiastics' to refrain from public controversy. It warned against undenominational instruction (a reference to the optional use of agreed selections from the Bible) and advised endeavours to obtain from the government 'a better order of things and more equitable conditions', but it referred also to 'the gratitude due to the British Parliament', and pointed out that 'since the introduction of this system of education, the Catholic religion does not appear to have sustained any injury' (for a fuller summary of this *Rescript of His Holiness Pope Gregory XVI* see Murphy, 1959, 138-9). The immediate danger therefore passed. But in Liverpool, when the Conservatives regained power in 1841, they were faced with the need to act upon their electoral pledges to modify the arrangements in the Corporation Schools. They did not restore the *status quo*, making the use of the Anglican catechism compulsory, but insisted upon the reading of the Authorized Version. The Roman Catholic clergy asked that children might be allowed to attend for secular instruction only, but this was refused. Thereupon the Roman Catholic children were withdrawn from the schools.

It seemed that Lord Ashley was right when, after the failure of Graham's endeavours in 1843, he wrote, with obvious satisfaction, '"United education" is an impossibility. It ought never again to be attempted' (Parker, 1907, I, 345).

3

'Progress by administration'

Kay-Shuttleworth and the Committee of Council on Education

The first secretary to the Committee of Council on Education, Dr
James Phillips Kay, was an extremely able administrator. He had
been, among other things, a Sunday school superintendent, a
doctor in charge of a cholera hospital in Manchester, a writer on
*The Moral and Physical Condition of the Working Classes Employed
in the Cotton Manufacture in Manchester*, and an Assistant Poor
Law Commissioner; he had studied educational systems abroad,
had been concerned at home with the provision of education for
pauper children and had undertaken practical experiments to
improve the training of teachers. He represented a new and necessary factor in the government of a modern state: the high civil
servant, well-briefed, semi-permanent and therefore in a position to
advise ministers new to their tasks – and to survive their fall. He
was, above all, able to propose policies of the highest political
importance as being inevitable consequences of existing precedents
and commitments, right reasoning and the impartial, expert study
of the facts.

Kay-Shuttleworth (to give him the name which he adopted in
1842) had earlier favoured the united education of children of all
sects, but the opposition aroused to Russell's proposals in 1839
had convinced him that the education of the poor must remain
associated with the separate churches – though he preferred to use
the term 'religious communions', lest he be thought to refer only
to the clergy – and he publicly declared that 'the feuds of sects
and the interests of bodies incompetent effectually to deal with this
national question should not rob the people of a national system
of education' (1839, 40). He was activated by three main beliefs:
that much better and more extensive provision must be made for
the education of the poor, and therefore much greater assistance
must be provided by the state; that increased state aid must involve
increased state control of secular instruction, this being desirable
not merely to ensure efficiency but because the state was in the

best position to gather and spread information about desirable reforms; that whilst religious instruction should remain the province of the clergy the general supervision of the school should be shared with the laity, this in practice to involve, wherever possible, supervision of the secular education by a lay majority.

In 1843 Kay-Shuttleworth wrote privately to Russell of the government's decision in 1839 to 'assert the claims of the civil power to the control of the education of the country'; this, he claimed, had been done 'effectually' by the establishment of the Committee of Council (Smith, 1923, 147). But at first he had to tread extremely carefully and assure suspicious critics that alarm concerning the functions of the Committee was 'groundless', these being 'precisely similar to those which were exercised by the Treasury' in previous years (1839, 50). Since the Treasury had never even enforced its rights to call upon the aided schools for 'periodical reports', this was to claim very little. But Kay-Shuttleworth was aware that whatever progress had so far been made (the grants in aid of school building, the inauguration of the national system in Ireland, the creation of the Committee of Council) had come not from formal legislation but from annual parliamentary grants and administrative decrees. Now that he considered himself to be 'in a responsible position with respect to the first steps towards the construction of a national system of education', he felt that 'the way could be prepared by administration' (1877 MS., quoted Smith, 1923, 88). It is remarkable that, in spite of all the thunder of the Conservative opposition to the establishment of the Committee in 1839, Peel was of the same opinion when, in 1842, in a letter marked 'most private', he wrote to Graham: 'My own belief is that a more rapid advance in promoting good education will be made by the cautious and gradual extension of the power and pecuniary means of the Committee of the Privy Council, than by the announcement of any plan by the government' (Parker, 1899, II, 533).

The 'Concordat' of 1840

Flushed with their triumph in preventing the establishment of the state training college and model school in 1839, and angered by their failure to destroy the Committee of Council, the Anglican authorities were in no mood to accept interference from the state. Resistance was greatly strengthened by the growing influence of the Tractarian (Oxford) movement. Just when the Established Church was being called upon (even by many of its own members) to relinquish claims for special consideration based upon its close connection with the state, what to many was a much more appealing doctrine was now being spread abroad; this emphasized that, as one Anglican historian has put it, 'the Church is a Divine Society and not a department of State' (Vidler, 1949, 122) – as often in recent years it had appeared to be. The state, it was now proclaimed, ought to assist the church, but must in no way seek to control it. Moreover, as education was part of the mission of the church, two consequences followed: (a) there could be no separation of secular from religious instruction (it was sometimes debated whether teachers ought not at least to be in minor Holy Orders (Maurice, 1839, 363-4); (b) the rôle of the state must be limited to providing material and financial assistance. Since these and other Tractarian beliefs (e.g. the emphasis on apostolic succession and the exalted function of the priest) appealed to many of the clergy, and particularly to many of those who took their calling and the work of the church in education most seriously, they had a considerable influence on the deliberations and policies of the National Society. Many even of those suspicious of Tractarian teachings were glad to see the rôle of the church so strongly defended in a time of danger and could not risk the reproach of being lukewarm in her cause.

The Committee of Council had bravely proposed in 1839 to modify the regulations governing the payment of grants, to allow these to be made: (a) 'in particular cases', for the 'support' as well as the building of schools; (b) for schools in 'very poor and populous districts' where the amount of public contribution hitherto demanded could not be obtained; and (c), again 'in particular cases', where the application did not come through the National or British Societies. For a time little could be done to implement these proposed changes. But, more important, the Committee also recommended that no further grant should be made 'unless the right of inspection be retained, in order to secure a conformity to the regulations and discipline established in the several schools, with such improvements as may from time to time be suggested by the Committee' (M.C.C., 1839-40, viii). The Committee here was clearly on very weak ground, with its political support as yet extremely insecure and its demand for permanent inspection based on a single initial grant of (at most) half the building cost.

The National Society determined to resist this first attempt of the state 'to assert the claims of the civil power' in respect of elementary education. Of 204 grants already promised by the government only thirty-five were accepted when the provision regarding inspection was published (N.S.R., 1840). After much angry discussion the Committee of Council had to accept many of the Anglican clergy's demands. The Committee agreed to issue instructions to its (or, more precisely, Her Majesty's) inspectors emphasizing that inspection 'was not intended as a means of exercising control, but of affording assistance'; the inspector's rôle was to obtain and convey information and to encourage local efforts, he 'having no power to interfere' or 'to offer any advice or information excepting where it is invited' (*M.C.C.*, 1839-40, 22-24). In what was clearly intended to be not merely an instruction but a formal undertaking and a pledge, the Committee declared that they were 'strongly of the opinion that no plan of education ought to be encouraged in which intellectual instruction is not subordinate to the regulation of the thoughts and habits of the children by the doctrines and precepts of revealed religion' (ibid., 24). (It was eventually made a condition of grant that the Authorized Version should be read daily.)

The provisions concerning the inspection of religious instruction were stated in an Order of Council issued in August 1840 and often later referred to as the 'Concordat'. In accordance with their contention that secular and religious instruction must be inseparable, the Anglican authorities insisted that inspectors of Church of England Schools should concern themselves with both. The Archbishops of York and Canterbury, each with regard to his own province, should be consulted about any appointments as inspectors of Anglican schools (these, in fact, were initially Anglican clergymen); the archbishops could even suggest candidates and ensure the dismissal of inspectors eventually considered by them to be unsuitable. The general instructions to inspectors would be 'communicated' to the archbishops before being sanctioned by the Committee of Council, and those concerning the inspection of religious instruction were to be drawn up by the archbishops themselves. Copies of an inspector's report on a school must be sent to the appropriate archbishop and bishop. The existing system of relating grants to voluntary subscriptions favoured the Anglicans, who therefore now insisted that the principle should be formally re-affirmed. Clearly, what had been intended as a move towards state control had become, in the eyes of the Anglican authorities, partly a government-financed means of ensuring efficient religious instruction (all the more striking since religious instruction in the British Society's schools was not to be inspected, and even the right to consultation about an inspector's appointment was not conceded until 1843 though this had been granted to the Church of Scotland since 1840). Not surprisingly, the first inspector of Anglican schools appointed, the Rev. John Allen, at first considered himself to be primarily responsible to the Church of England, and was only with difficulty persuaded, in connection with the submission of reports, that inspectors were to be in fact the servants of the Crown. The National Society even hoped (in vain) that inspection would be extended to schools not receiving government grants. (In Scotland, however, where the need for state aid was less pressing, those in charge of the majority of schools preferred to decline the grants rather than accept the conditions laid down by the Committee of Council.)

As a modern historian of the National Society has observed 'the Concordat of 1840 represents the high-water mark of the Church's power in the struggle who was to determine educational policy' (Burgess, 1958, 90). Nevertheless, the principle of state inspection was established, much to the disgust of its more extreme opponents, and particularly of the Tractarians Archdeacon Manning and the Rev. G. A. Denison: the latter was among the numerous supporters of schools (clerical and lay) who rejected state grants rather than submit to inspection.

The Tractarians

But it soon became obvious that Kay-Shuttleworth had every reason to welcome the opposition of the Tractarians, particularly as this was voiced by Denison. State aid divorced from state control for the schools of a single church implied for most thinking people a combination of old-fashioned political and religious intolerance with economic heresy. The High Church Rev. W. F. Hook denounced the proposal as 'monstrous' (Stephens, 1881, 347), and it was obvious that in the world of political action Newman's ideas were unlikely to prevail over Bentham's. The importance ascribed to the powers and functions of the priesthood alienated many laymen, particularly politicians in all parties and landowning subscribers unaccustomed to such pretensions from parsons. The emphasis on apostolic succession naturally angered Nonconformist ministers, especially Methodists. All this, and the Tractarians' general drift towards sympathy with Roman Catholic doctrines, aroused hostility and suspicion among Nonconformists and Evangelical Anglicans.

Thus, whatever proposals Kay-Shuttleworth made to extend secular power he could be sure would be hotly debated, and perhaps successfully opposed, by the National Society, but in such terms that he would win considerable support elsewhere.

The Voluntaryists

Their successful opposition to Graham's proposals of 1843 had assured the Nonconformists of their strength, and a new factor was now added to the 'religious problem'. It had long been a tradition of the Congregationalists, Baptists and many other Nonconformists that the state should not intervene in religious affairs, and of course resentment of penal sanctions and of the privileges of the 'state' church had reinforced this belief. Since it was considered axiomatic that education must include religious instruction, the question arose whether state grants for schools might be accepted. Many Nonconformists, and not merely the Wesleyans, established schools without seeking state assistance, but suspicion of the state diminished after 1827, for, by extending their civil liberties and removing some of their grievances against the Established Church, the state had appeared briefly in the rôle of a protector. Nevertheless the willingness of Nonconformists to support the British Society, in spite of its acceptance of government grants from 1833, was not regarded as a breach of the principle that there must be no state support for religious teaching: it could plausibly be argued that subscribers to the society were concerned about the education not of their own children but of children of all sects, and that in any case no part of the state grant in aid of building was spent on religious instruction. Again, most Nonconformists (except the Wesleyans) had welcomed Russell's proposals in 1839; a meeting of the 'Ministers of the Three Denominations' (mainly Congregational and Baptist ministers of London) had been able both to express support and, since Nonconformist chaplains to the Normal School would not have been paid, to emphasize the principle that 'if any portion of the public money be granted' for educational purposes 'it should be for the advancement of that secular education concerning which we are all agreed, and not for education in religion, on which we are so much divided' (Dale, R. W., 1907, 652).

But the Church of England's opposition to the proposals of 1839, the 'Concordat' of 1840, and Graham's Bill of 1843 convinced many Nonconformists, and especially most leaders of the Congregationalists and Baptists, that the 'state' church would always be favoured, and this encouraged a reaction towards rejecting all state control of education: unlike the Tractarians, they accepted the corollary that this involved also rejecting all state assistance. The leaders of this 'Voluntaryist' movement were Edward Baines, the Congregationalist editor of the *Leeds Mercury*, and Edward Miall. From 1843 the former eloquently denounced the evil of paying taxes to disseminate religious doctrines believed to be false, and praised the virtues of independence, competition, variety, self-reliance, parental responsibility and political and religious freedom, all of which, he maintained, would be endangered if the state supported and controlled education; whilst Miall, a Congregational minister and a Radical, expounded similar views in the pages of his journal *The Nonconformist*. In 1844 Miall founded the Anti-

State-Church Society, later known as the Society for the Liberation of Religion from State Control.

Thus Kay-Shuttleworth found that potential allies he badly needed, who had supported Russell in 1839, had become extremely active and outspoken opponents. The 'education question' had become merely a part of a much more general contest, involving controversy not merely about the existence and rights of a 'state' church, but about the new identity which many Anglicans (the majority by no means extremists) were struggling to establish for their church, this involving serious misgivings about the powers of the state to intervene in spiritual affairs. And all this was to be accompanied by suspicion and hostility among Protestants about doctrinal differences which had long been in abeyance.

The 'management clauses'

The support of the Conservative government from 1841 ensured the continuance of the Committee of Council. The funds available to it were increased, grants were made available for school furniture and apparatus, and towards the cost of building training colleges and teachers' houses; additional inspectors were appointed. But the return to power of the Liberals in 1846 led to much more rapid development. The Committee now sought to reduce the powers of the clergy in respect of individual church schools. The rules of the National Society did not insist upon lay membership of the managing boards of schools, though they allowed for it: they did provide that control of religious instruction should rest with the clergy, with a right of appeal to the bishop where managers disagreed. In practice the vast majority of Anglican schools had no management committees and, often because of the apathy of the laity, 'were under the exclusive superintendence of the clergy' (quoted Burgess, 1958, 148).

The National Society had already indicated the desirability of obtaining more lay co-operation when the Committee of Council put forward model trust deeds to be adopted by schools built with state assistance. These varied to meet local conditions, and permitted the clergyman to be the sole manager where populations were small and suitable lay managers were not available, but in general the management clauses, as amended after discussion, would require: (a) that lay managers would serve with the clergy on managing boards: they would usually be elected from, and by, subscribers, but might in some cases be nominated by the clergyman and thereafter elect their own successors; (b) that whilst the control of religious instruction (including the appointment and dismissal of teachers on religious grounds) would rest with the clergy, the control of the secular instruction would lie with all the managers, clergy and laymen alike, who, of course, would all be members of the appropriate religious communion. Since disputes might arise as to which *were* secular and which religious matters, detailed arrangements were laid down for arbitration not, as hitherto, by the bishop alone, or even by clergy and laymen, as such, but by representatives of the church and of the state. The issue was largely one of principle, since state 'intervention' could only arise where the clerical and lay co-religionists disagreed (and the state 'representative' would, in practice, usually be the clergy-man initially appointed as inspector with the approval of an archbishop, and liable to dismissal at his request); but the principle was obviously an important one. Further, the Committee of Council was clearly determined to defend the right of lay managers to control secular education, and, in particular, to prevent the dismissal of teachers by the clergy on grounds other than religious.

The imposition of this new regulation by the state, and the consequences anticipated from it, aroused extraordinary bitterness. Denison insisted that there could be no separation between secular and religious education, that 'control over the entire *order, teaching,* and *discipline* of the school and over the appointment and dismissal of teachers, should be in the hands of the local clergy with appeal only to the Bishop' (Denison, L. E., 1902, 16). He was supported in particular by many Tractarians and other High Church clergymen. The National Society eventually reduced its claims to a request that the management rules might be decided upon by the school founders and not by the state. But many Anglicans considered the Committee of Council's line a reasonable one: these included the Bishop of Salisbury and of course many laymen, among them Gladstone, who in 1852 rejected 'the doctrine that the founders of these [state-aided] schools have the right to arrange their management as they please and free from Government control' (*Hansard*, CCXXII, 1109). In the event, no final agreement was reached and the National Society refused to recommend the adoption of the new management clauses to those establishing schools. But the Committee of Council had no difficulty in enforcing its rules in respect of new schools requiring aid, insisting somewhat bluntly that 'the broadest distinction exists between schools which owe their origin solely to private benefactors and those the establishment of which is largely aided by the State' (*M.C.C.*, 1847-8, I, xcvi).

It may be convenient to note here that when Lord Derby's government in 1852 altered the management clauses to permit the clergy to dismiss teachers on 'moral' as well as religious grounds there was a great outcry from many teachers in church schools;

shortly afterwards, on their return to power, the Liberal government cancelled the new provision as one which would 'degrade
and lower the condition of every schoolmaster' (Tropp, 1957, 49).

The Minutes of 1846

In 1846 the resources, and therefore the powers, of the Committee
of Council were greatly increased. The existing system of elementary education was based almost entirely on the monitorial system,
and the inadequacy of this had become recognized on all sides.
Yet its abolition would obviously create immense difficulties for
the supporters of voluntary schools, since more classrooms, more
training colleges, more teachers and more money to pay them
would be required.

Kay-Shuttleworth saw that 'if there were to be one teacher
for every twenty-five scholars, an army of teachers would be
needed' (Smith, 1923, 90), and in 1846 the Committee of Council
published minutes embodying his plans to increase the number of
teachers and improve their training. Selected children in the schools
would become salaried pupil teachers, with schoolmasters paid
to instruct them; pupil teachers who passed an examination would
be given grants (Queen's Scholarships) towards their maintenance
in training colleges, and grants would also be paid to the training
colleges at the end of each successful year of training. The trained
teacher would receive from the state an annual sum (dependent
on the length of his training) as part of his salary, if the school
managers paid at least twice as much in addition and provided
a free house. After at least fifteen years' service in inspected schools,
certain teachers would be eligible for retirement pensions from the
state. It was later agreed that untrained teachers in inspected
schools would be able to qualify for the state augmentation of
salary.

All of this involved increased inspection and examination by the
state. Only schools suitably equipped and staffed were permitted
to train pupil-teachers, who were examined at the end of each
year, then for the Queen's Scholarship, and again at the end of
each year in the training college; untrained serving teachers seeking the special grants were examined; the augmentation of salary
was paid only if the teacher served in a school certified by an
inspector as efficient. Subjects for examination were 'minutely
prescribed' in the minutes of the Committee of Council (Kay-
Shuttleworth, 1853, 75): 'My Lords' of the Committee might express 'a preference on behalf of the first three books of Euclid',
or decide that women students would not be required 'to answer
questions in Vulgar fractions or decimals' (M.C.C., 1850-1, I,

xviii). Obviously all this involved an immense extension, not only of state expenditure, and of direct payments to individuals, but of lasting control and influence over secular education, based upon continued annual support.

The grants to Wesleyans, Roman Catholics and others

In spite of some protests, the National and British Societies welcomed the increased assistance and accepted the new controls, but of course augmented aid for them involved still greater injustice to those receiving no help at all. The Wesleyans for a time came close to continuing independent: although they had supported the Anglicans against Russell's proposals in 1839 they had joined with other Nonconformists in 1843 to oppose the special favour shown by Graham to the Established Church, and had adopted the Voluntaryist position. In 1847, however, they agreed to accept state aid on being assured that this would not preclude their opposing similar assistance for Roman Catholic schools. The principles of joint clerical and lay management of schools they already practised. The Committee of Council were obviously pleased to announce that 'the Model Deeds of Schools in Union with the British and Foreign School Society, the Wesleyan Connexion, and the Free Church of Scotland ... confide the supreme and undivided power of executing the School Trusts to a simple majority of the School Committee' (M.C.C., 1850-51, I, xxxviii).

The Roman Catholic policy had hardened since the events of 1839-43. When Roman Catholic children were withdrawn from the Liverpool Corporation Schools in 1842, having been refused permission to attend for secular education alone, they had been marched in procession to a new Roman Catholic school, which, from shortage of funds, it had taken a decade to complete. The gesture was symbolic: henceforward the Roman Catholic authorities were convinced that no acceptable compromise would be forthcoming, so that they must be prepared to rely on their own efforts and insist on having their own schools. Within a decade the newly established hierarchy was declaring: 'No congregation should be allowed to remain without its schools.... Indeed, whereever there may seem to be an opening for a new mission, we should prefer the erection of a school so arranged as to serve temporarily as a chapel, to that of a church, without one ... it is the good school that secures the virtuous and edifying congregation' (quoted Diamond, 1963, 55). When the Roman Catholic authorities applied for state aid in 1846, this was at first refused by the Liberals on the ground that the regulations of the Committee of Council required the reading of the Authorized Version in the schools assisted. The desire not to rekindle controversy just before a general election was understandable, if unheroic. But for some influential Liberals and Conservatives 'reasons of state', as well as human sympathy, dictated a more courageous course. In 1845, in spite of intense opposition, Peel had put the state grant to Maynooth on a permanent basis, and Gladstone had quixotically resigned from the government because, in spite of views proclaimed earlier, he now agreed with this. Peel knew the condition of the children of the Roman Catholic poor and argued that to leave them 'immersed in ignorance' would harm 'the Protestant community' (*Hansard*, XCI, 1231). In spite of considerable opposition, state aid for Roman Catholic schools was sanctioned in 1847, and the Catholic Poor School Committee was set up to communicate with the Committee of Council.

The extraordinary sensitivity of the consciences of those with whom the state had to deal at this time may be briefly illustrated thus : since the requirement that the Authorized Version be read in grant-aided schools had now been withdrawn to accommodate the Roman Catholics, and since none of the church authorities except the Anglicans could conscientiously accept the state inspection of religious instruction, the state would be unable to demonstrate that it was not subsidizing purely secular instruction. It therefore proposed that school managers themselves might present to inspectors certificates that the religious instruction given was 'satisfactory', only to meet with protests from the Free Church of Scotland that 'by *requiring* and *accepting* as satisfactory the certificates of managers of any religious persuasion (Popish or Socinian as well as Protestant and Evangelical) the government appears to act upon the principle of indiscriminately supporting religious truth and error alike'. The government therefore resignedly arranged to make it clear in the regulations governing grants to Roman Catholic (and later to Jewish) schools that inspectors would ask for no assurance about religious instruction (*M.C.C.*, 1847-8, I, lxii).

It soon became clear that the Roman Catholic representatives would forgo grant rather than yield on certain principles. The inspector of their schools must be a Roman Catholic. The same provisions would apply regarding consultation before the appointment of the inspector and the restriction of his activity to secular education as had been agreed with the British Society and the Church of Scotland, and now with the Wesleyans and the Free Church of Scotland (though the Church of England remained the only body able to propose candidates and ensure the dismissal of inspectors considered unsatisfactory). The Catholic Poor School Committee was opposed to the principle of lay management even of 'the temporal affairs of their schools' but accepted it under protest, since it was not 'actually contrary to Catholic doctrine' and had been insisted upon for other religious bodies (*M.C.C.*, 1850-1, I, xxxiv-v). But they refused uncompromisingly to depart from their contention that only the clergy could decide what did or did not fall within the sphere of religion and therefore within their sole jurisdiction. Lacking the support of any lay Roman Catholic opinion, the Committee of Council, much to the disgust of some Anglicans, had to concede that the only appeal on such disputed points must be to a bishop.

The single-school area and the 'conscience clause'

More than twenty years after the minutes of 1846 were issued Kay-Shuttleworth claimed that they had drawn 'every religious communion, except the Congregational Dissenters and bodies allied with them, into co-operation with the Government, and created a vast denominational system which firmly established popular education on a religious basis' (1868, 8). The exception, however, was an important one. The great extension of state expenditure and control naturally angered the Voluntaryists, now called upon to subsidize the teaching of Anglican or 'Popish' doctrines by paying taxes not merely for school building but for the training and payment of the teachers. They even formed a political group to contest some parliamentary elections in 1847 and claimed to be responsible for the defeat of T. B. Macaulay at Edinburgh. The Liberals had flouted both the conscientious scruples and the economic views of many of their Nonconformist supporters: Baines considered Russell inconsistent to speak of protection as 'the bane of Agriculture' without applying the doctrine to education (1846, 5). By 1851 the Voluntaryists were confident in their strength: since 1843 they had built, entirely without state assistance, 364 schools and a training college (Homerton). Like other Nonconformists they were delighted when the religious census of 1851 pointed to the fact that 'in gross the dissenting churches commanded the allegiance of nearly half the population of England and Wales': on its publication Miall said that 'as a dissenter he felt like the son of a peer, treated from birth as a menial, and suddenly finding himself ... recognised and receiving the attention due to his rank' (Chadwick, 1966, 367-8).

But the supporters of the denominational system of education were also confident, and, with state aid, considerable progress was being made. The Church of England was strengthened by reforms and more conscious of her spiritual functions; the Roman Catholic Church had 'restored' its hierarchy in 1850, and its clergy became so convinced of the evils of 'united education' that in 1867, with the approval of the Vatican, its bishops virtually forbade Roman

Catholics to attend Oxford and Cambridge universities, by that time open to them (Evennett, 1950, 299). It might have seemed that the efforts of Denominationalists and Voluntaryists, with or without state assistance, would eventually produce a national system of elementary education. But there were three principal obstacles to progress: (a) the problem of single-school areas; (b) the difficulty, if the state was not itself to provide and wholly support schools, of having them built and maintained where they were most needed; (c) the great expenditure and immense administrative machinery certain to be required as a national system developed. We must briefly consider each of these.

The problem of the single-school area was referred to in chapter 2 as one obvious objection to a denominational system of national education. It could be alleviated for parents who rejected the particular faith taught in the only available school by permitting withdrawal from religious instruction and worship on conscientious grounds, preferably by the insertion into the trust deeds of the school of what became known as a 'conscience clause' formally agreeing to this. The Committee of Council was in favour of such clauses almost from its inception but was not strong enough to insist on their adoption as a condition of receiving aid, especially as most of the schools concerned were connected with the Established Church. When the Wesleyans were granted state aid in 1847, the Committee welcomed their assurance that they did not in their schools insist upon attendance for denominational instruction or worship, and regretted that the National Society would not similarly 'recognise the state of the law as to the toleration of diversities in religious belief' (M.C.C., 1846, 23). The Roman Catholic authorities could not accept any separation between secular and religious instruction and rather astutely quoted from the Committee's own minute at the time of Russell's proposals of 1839, requiring that 'religion be combined with the whole matter of instruction and regulate the entire system of education'; nevertheless they agreed to permit withdrawal on conscientious grounds from 'catechetical instruction on the doctrines and practices of the Catholic Church' (Diamond, 1963, 48).

From its foundation, some members of the National Society had felt that 'the true spirit and policy of the Church of England' should be 'comprehension and not exclusion' (quoted Best, 1956, 166). Later a Wesleyan critic admitted that, especially in those Anglican schools receiving state aid, 'the management was often more liberal' than the National Society's regulations laid down (Rigg, 1873, 145). But acceptance of a 'conscience clause' implied officially restricting religious instruction to set times, and hence its separation from secular instruction, a principle hotly denounced by many

Anglicans and particularly by the Tractarians, led, once again, by Denison. The bitter disputes on the conscience (as on the management) clauses shocked even many observers sympathetic to the church and led to a fall in subscriptions to the National Society (Burgess, 1958, 213); the High Church clergyman F. D. Maurice complained that 'the poor children are passed by while we are fighting' (Maurice, F., 1885, I, 547). The 'fighting' was all the more acrimonious because its causes ran deeper than the issue of the schools. A particular source of resentment was the current use of the Judicial Committee of the Privy Council as the ultimate court of appeal in ecclesiastical cases, so that lay lawyers could and did rule upon the doctrine of the Church of England on such matters as baptism. Numbers of High Church Anglicans were divided even within themselves as to whether to demand disestablishment in order to avoid supporting a 'House of Parliament Church'; but on the question of the schools they could unite.

Many Evangelical Anglicans, resenting the 'Romanizing' tendencies of the Tractarians and their intolerance towards Protestant Dissenters in their schools, organized the Church Education Society, which favoured acceptance of the 'conscience clause'. Thereupon a coalition government in 1854 readily took advantage of this manifest disunity to abolish one remaining anachronistic 'privilege' of the Established Church: it refused to advise the queen to issue any more Royal Letters asking for financial support for the National Society (Burgess, 1958, 213). Some of the clergy were well aware, as one of them put it, 'that it was no light matter to talk, as some now do, of severing all connection with the civil power, and of throwing ourselves upon the independent support of churchmen': he told them that a special appeal for funds in 1843, 'at a crisis of political and religious excitement, had not been so successful as to invite a repetition' (Hamilton, 1850, 50). In 1852 nearly 3,000 Anglicans, most of them clergymen, petitioned the committee of the National Society, asking that 'A more cordial co-operation with the state in promoting the education of the poor than is now apparent should be forthwith resumed, entirely confiding in the disposition of the Committee of Council to exact no condition of which the Church can reasonably complain' (Kay-Shuttleworth, 1853, 21). The Tractarians were by now much discredited by the conversion to Roman Catholicism of Newman and Manning, and in 1853 Kay-Shuttleworth felt strong enough to deride them as 'the medieval party', quoting their most extreme claims (not forgetting those made earlier by Manning) as being manifestly absurd. When Denison failed in his attempt to have Gladstone defeated at an election at Oxford in 1853 (because of the latter's membership of the Committee of Council) his influence abruptly declined.

But the National Society felt unable to sanction officially the separation of religious and secular education, and refused to support and transmit applications for building grants where a 'conscience clause' was accepted. The state, therefore, felt obliged to intervene. Kay-Shuttleworth had resigned in 1849 because of ill health, and his successor, R. R. W. Lingen, was determined to settle the issue. Tentative moves from 1852, suggesting that exemption from denominational instruction might be sanctioned by a bishop, came to nothing, and from 1860 the Committee of Council began refusing building grants for proposed Anglican schools in what would become single-school areas unless the trust deeds contained a 'conscience clause'. Once again, as with the management clauses, the state had imposed its decision on the Established Church, but only with respect to a limited number of new schools; and the troublesome problem of the single-school area remained to strengthen objections to a wholly denominational policy.

Problems of expense and administration

It is difficult to assess the relative financial contributions of the churches and the state to elementary education during the nineteenth century, for the many schools which did not qualify for grant rarely figured in statistical returns. It is, of course, certain that subscriptions and gifts of land by clergy and laity at first dwarfed the payments made by the state: between 1833 and 1844, even in respect of schools which did receive government grants, the contribution of the state was apparently only of the order of 30 per cent (M.C.C., 1844, I, 121). But the policy begun with the minutes of 1846 had vastly increased the government expenditure, and from 1853 in rural areas and 1856 in large towns 'capitation' grants were paid in respect of each child making a given number of attendances at schools satisfactorily staffed and run, if they were supported also by adequate voluntary contributions and school pence. (The qualifications are important, since they obviously limited the expenditure entailed.) In 1861 it was calculated that in England the annual cost of teaching a pupil in a state-assisted Anglican school was about £1 8s. 0d. (excluding rent and government administrative expenses), of which the state paid about 11s. 2d. Fees supplied 'a proportion of the total income of the schools, varying from about a quarter to as much as three-fifths' (N.C., I, 71), but normally, it would seem, they amounted to about one-third (e.g. R.S.P.C., 1870, 174). In England there were in 1859 thirty-four training colleges receiving government aid: the state paid about 31 per cent of the cost of providing them and was currently furnishing about 64 per cent of their income – as much as

76 per cent in the case of Anglican colleges for men (N.C., I, 646). Only two colleges (at Homerton and Lichfield) were independent of state aid. The annual government grant for elementary education and teacher training had risen from the original £20,000 twenty-six years earlier to £836,920; it had actually increased more than five-fold in the past seven years. The current position appeared disturbing, and future prospects positively alarming, so that the state was anxious to find some means of reducing the financial burden.

Furthermore, one result of the rather informal way in which the Committee of Council had (of necessity) sidled into existence was that it had no administrative framework capable of dealing efficiently even with existing commitments. Until 1856 its links with parliament were tenuous: its annual expenditure and minutes might be discussed and questions asked of the Home Secretary, but it was not until that year that a responsible parliamentary 'head of department' was appointed – a vice-president of the Committee of Council who would be a member of the government. (The Lord President of the Privy Council was, *ex officio*, at least nominally president of all its committees.) The Committee of Council was now to take over superintendence of the work of the Science and Art Department (hitherto assigned to the Board of Trade); the administrative duties were to be exercised by an Education Department. These duties were ridiculously extensive: the task of calculating grants payable in respect of individual teachers and children was alone formidable, and coping with the managers of many thousands of separate schools was such an immense task that long delays were inevitable.

The deficiency in educational provision

Despite the much increased state grants, great numbers of children were still not being taught. According to the Newcastle Commission, 'one of the chief failures' of the existing system was that it 'did not touch the districts which require most assistance': there were 'immense tracts of the country' where state assistance was unknown (I, 316-7). Prevailing economic theory encouraged the convenient practice of making grants only where adequate voluntary subscriptions and parental contributions were forthcoming and schools were well staffed and conducted: with the result that the children of the poorest districts, and those with the poorest or most feckless parents, were least likely to have schools, whilst the least efficient schools earned the lowest grants, if any. The churches were unable to cope with rapidly changing needs caused by movements of population into cities or out to their suburbs. Children of 'respectable' working-class parents were withdrawn by them from schools which admitted the most destitute and brutalized children of the slums: these were almost totally neglected apart from some efforts made by the Ragged Schools, some Roman Catholic organizations and (later) some Ritualist priests (*R.S.P.C.*, 1870, 174; Bowen, 1968, 291). Yet the state had not the will or the power or (it believed) the resources to provide schools where needed, to compel attendance, or, as a corollary to this, to provide education free. Whatever 'progress by administration' had achieved, the combined contributions of church and state were still hopelessly inadequate.

Local aid and control

Long before 1870 it was clear to most of those anxious to make national provision for the education of the working classes that these difficulties caused by expense, over-stretched administration and the inequitable and inadequate distribution of schools must be dealt with by supplementing state aid with local finance, local effort and local control. The years from 1847 to 1867 saw repeated attempts to make this possible. But the new proposals raised difficulties of their own. The Denominationalists felt that they had as much right as anyone to support from the rates, but feared the consequences of local control: Anglicans had no wish to be at the mercy of the Nonconformists and Radicals of Birmingham, or Roman Catholics to suffer from local religious hostility in Liverpool or Wales. On the other hand, most convinced Nonconformists, and especially, of course, the Voluntaryists, felt extremely strongly about paying rates to support religious instruction, particularly religious instruction which they felt, in the case of the Established Church, to be unwanted by most of its recipients, and, in the case of the 'Church of Rome', to be pernicious. If adherents of the Church of England were not prepared to support it they should not, as with the hated church-rate, call upon Nonconformists to save it. Moreover there was something particularly personal about the payment of rates: it was easier to recognize their destined purpose, more practicable than in the case of national taxes (almost all indirect) for the objector to withhold his payment – and conscience might therefore urge him to do so. Again, there was the problem not only of the degree of local control but of who should exercise it. Outside the large towns there was only the most rudimentary provision for local government and the vestries and magistrates mainly responsible for it were almost everywhere under the influence of landowners likely to support the Established Church. Most Nonconformists who favoured local support wanted to have local boards elected by the ratepayers for the specific purpose of helping to provide, maintain and control schools.

With all these causes for dispute added to the perpetual 'religious difficulty' it is hardly surprising that for a generation attempts at legislation so miserably failed.

Attempts at legislation

It is not possible, and fortunately not necessary, to detail here all of those attempts between 1847 and 1868, but they can be reviewed in general terms. In the main they were directed to coping in one way or another with the problems just described, arising from the desire to call upon local administration and support; but of course there was also the need to decide what should happen to existing schools and what provision should be permitted for religious instruction both in them and in any schools set up under the proposed new policy. The weakness of the denominational system, because of its exclusiveness and inadequate resources, was manifest, and neither central nor local governments were likely to accept the plea of the future Cardinal Vaughan that the state should simply provide 'more largely' for all the different sects (Vaughan, 1868, 34). Yet the Denominationalists had their existing schools (to whose support the state seemed committed), great moral and political influence and a strong defensive position. Their opponents could call upon much ability and considerable skill in organization but they were divided by the Voluntaryist movement and other sources of disunity.

The Radicals in general demanded that elementary education should be universal, compulsory, free, supported from local rates with popular control and secular. Most of those now and later who advocated purely secular education had definite religious beliefs (many, indeed, were Nonconformist ministers) and hoped that religious teaching would be given separately. The High Church Vicar of Leeds, the Rev. W. F. Hook, wrote in support of such an arrangement (1846). But the policy aroused much suspicion and hostility, and not only from Denominationalists. The Lancashire Public School Association, founded in 1847 to promote the Radical programme, became in 1850 the National Public School Association. Its leading supporters included Cobden, Bright and others able to contribute extensive experience of organizing public agitation from their successful campaign against the Corn Laws. It won support from many Nonconformists and liberal Anglicans, but at a price. Cobden, who was prepared to accept almost any workable solution to the religious problem, knew English public opinion well, including that among the working classes; with considerable difficulty he prevailed upon the national association at its foundation not to use the word 'secular' in its title and to think of its policy rather as favouring 'unsectarian' religious instruction (Jones, 1967, 304). This made it possible to broaden the association's appeal but alienated the Voluntaryists still further, and raised the controversial questions not only whether religious instruction should be unsectarian, but whether it could be: those given to theological discussion could readily demonstrate the difficulties, and the practical experience of the British Society was hardly conclusive, since it had not to cope with Roman Catholics and was constantly offending Unitarians (Binns, 1908, 152-5).

Naturally, the existing system was strongly defended. The London Committee of Friends of Voluntary Schools and the Manchester and Salford Committee on Education were particularly active in the early 1850s. Both sides produced parliamentary Bills, and, in the face of repeated failures, both made some concessions, as when the National Public School Association agreed to allow rate aid for denominational schools (in return for local control) and the Manchester and Salford Committee expressed willingness to accept a 'conscience clause' for schools assisted from the rates. There were proposals that the religious instruction in schools newly set up with rate support should be decided by the wishes of the majority in a given area, as in Sir John Pakington's Bill of 1855; that town councils should levy rates to be simply handed over to school managers; and even, from Kay-Shuttleworth, that the existing system should be strengthened by allowing ratepayers to indicate which denominational or other body they wished their payments to support. No agreement could be reached, and a government select committee achieved nothing. State intervention was no more successful: Lord John Russell's Borough Bill (1853) proposing that town councils might levy rates to assist existing schools had to be dropped, and the state was obliged to reinforce the current system in the usual way by issuing a minute of the Committee of Council: on this occasion capitation grants were made available to encourage regular attendance.

Even the state's urgent desire to economize could not force a solution. When the Newcastle Commission was appointed in 1858 to enquire into the state of public education and its possible extension there was a stipulation that this must be not only 'sound' but 'cheap'. The notorious system of 'payment by results' was inaugurated in 1862 to achieve these ends, and this, with other forms of retrenchment, including the cessation of building grants to training colleges, led to a temporary reduction in the annual education grant between 1862 and 1866 of more than 20 per cent. The system involved, of course, a considerable increase of state inspection and control, which was loudly denounced by Voluntaryists and Denominationalists alike. Kay-Shuttleworth himself objected that the existing co-operative relationship between church and state had been 'abruptly and harshly changed by the fiat of a Minister, without the consent of the great controlling bodies and communions, who have expended twice as much as the state. Even were Parliament to make such a change it would be a great national dishonour' (1861, 72). But the state was moved much more by the desire to reduce expenditure and increase efficiency than by any urge to extend its powers and curb the influence of the churches: this was shown (a) by the continuance of the 'Concordat' with the authorities of the Established Church, which meant that Anglican inspectors of Church of England schools could hold over managers and teachers the threat to refuse all or part of whatever grant was 'earned' by 'results' in other subjects if the religious instruction was deemed to be unsatisfactory; (b) by the new arrangements, made to cheapen and simplify administration, whereby payments to teachers were made through school managers, as if to emphasize that teachers were not civil servants; they often became, in effect, more dependent on the good will of the clergy.

It was clear that the state would consider quite intolerable the financial and administrative burdens which the creation of a national system of elementary education would involve. Recognizing this, a majority of the members of the Newcastle Commission recommended (1861) that state grants might be supplemented by local rates, but this came to nothing because of opposition to the proposal that the borough and county boards empowered to distribute the rates should be elected not by the ratepayers but by the town councils or quarter sessions.

Nevertheless by now the opposition to state intervention in the field of education, though still considerable, was weakening, and the state was becoming more aware of the need and more ready to act. The Voluntaryists on the Newcastle Commission, including Edward Miall, had made little more than a routine gesture when they claimed that 'in a country situated politically and socially as England is, Government has, ordinarily speaking, no educational duties, except towards those whom destitution, vagrancy, or crime casts upon its hands'. They felt that, since public interest had now been awakened and much educational provision made, the annual grants should be gradually withdrawn, though building grants should be continued in fairness to parishes which had so far not received help. However Miall and his fellows agreed, in view of existing circumstances, and 'on the rejection of their own view', to 'cordially adopt, in the second resort, the scheme of assistance approved by the majority of their colleagues' (I, 298-9).

Competition from abroad in trade and industry was demonstrating the weakness of a nation unable to base a system of secondary, technical and commercial education on the firm foundation of a national system of elementary education. In other areas of education the state was able to insist on reforms. In the face of bitter protests and obstruction, commissioners had been appointed to investigate the condition of Oxford and Cambridge universities, and consequent parliamentary action in 1854 and 1856 had inaugurated many changes, including the abolition of the religious tests which had prevented non-Anglicans from obtaining degrees (though not until 1871 was it possible for them to sit on the governing bodies of universities). The report of the Public Schools (Clarendon) Commission in 1864 led to revisions of the statutes and curricula of the leading public schools, to bring these somewhat more into line with modern needs. The Schools Inquiry (Taunton) Commission reported on the other endowed secondary schools (1868): the government recoiled from the recommendations which might have led to the establishment of a national system of secondary education supervised by provincial boards able to make use of existing endowments or even local rates, but the Endowed Schools Act (1869) did appoint commissioners authorized to revise the trust deeds of schools and it made possible the use of funds from obsolete charities for educational purposes. The commissioners were instructed that, when drawing up new statutes, they should abolish earlier regulations where these required teachers to be clergymen, should introduce a 'conscience clause', and should ensure that school governors would be chosen without reference to their religious beliefs. (The powers of the commissioners were transferred to the Charity Commission in 1874.) All this had involved trespassing on the independence of the universities and of public and other schools, and interference with the sacred right of long-dead property owners to have their testamentary instructions obeyed. The Industrial Schools Act of 1866 even accepted, for the limited number of children affected, the highly controversial principle that rate aid might be given to denominational schools. Factory Acts in 1864 and in 1867 extended the educational provisions of existing legislation. Yet the log jam regarding elementary education in general did not break.

In 1864 the Manchester Education Aid Society was formed to examine the educational condition of the city and help poor parents to pay fees; in 1867 the Birmingham Education Aid Society was founded with similar aims. The investigations of the two societies violently shook, without actually overthrowing, one of the most sacrosanct principles of almost all who had engaged in the conflict – that all but a small proportion of parents were able, and could be induced, to pay school fees. Their revelations demonstrated the need to provide free education, much to the concern of managers of voluntary schools: for official returns between 1851 and 1859 had shown that nearly 40 per cent of that part of their income not obtained from public funds had come from fees. The Manchester Education Bill Committee urged the government to establish a system of education which would be free, compulsory, rate-aided and locally controlled, existing schools to be assisted if a 'conscience clause' were accepted, but new schools to be unsectarian. For the Committee, H. A. Bruce, a former vice-president of the Committee of Council, supported by W. E. Forster, introduced bills in 1867 and 1868, again proposing that local boards might assist existing schools from the rates but also set up new schools, leaving decisions about religious instruction to the discretion of the boards.

These attempts again failed, but the climate was manifestly changing, needs becoming more obvious and the sense of frustration mounting. Even Kay-Shuttleworth, who had fought long and hard to defend the existing system, now reluctantly agreed that it was necessary 'to give to the Privy Council and to the provincial district a regulated and limited authority to take initiatory steps' instead of merely assisting schools as and where voluntary bodies chose to establish them (1868, 67). The same hard facts which had induced him to accept this increase in state 'interference' now led his old antagonists Edward Baines and Edward Miall, who had for a generation opposed all state intervention, support and control in the sphere of education, to admit defeat, so that the Voluntaryist movement collapsed. In 1867 Baines told his supporters in the Congregational Union that the conduct of practical men must be governed 'by facts and experience as well as by sacred principles'; public opinion had become less favourable and school committees and teachers were disheartened; subscriptions had declined; because of defections and school closures the Voluntaryists had no more schools than after the initial successful campaigns of 1843-6; 'in short, the purely voluntary system, which had done such immense service in former years, was obviously overmatched and undermined ... as educational voluntaries we are last in the field, and there is no dishonour in retreating before irresistible numbers' (1867, 3-8). He was now prepared to admit that, by refusing state support even for secular education, the Voluntaryists had 'overstrained a religious scruple', though religious instruction must never be financed or controlled by the state. Baines, with this proviso, henceforward favoured continued support for denominational schools, whilst Miall campaigned for purely secular schools;

but the principle of state support and control was no longer a live issue.

Even more indicative of changing ideas was the passing of the Reform Act of 1867. Robert Lowe was not alone in appreciating the need 'to compel our future masters to learn their letters' (*Hansard*, CLXXVIII, 1549). Kay-Shuttleworth was more specific when he spoke of 'the anti-social doctrines' held by the leaders of trades unions as to the relations between capital and labour, and their consequent organization to limit the freedom of workmen and masters by a system of terror; he described these as a warning to parliament of 'how much the law needs the support of sound economic opinions and higher moral principles among certain classes of workmen and how influential a general system of education might be in rearing a loyal, intelligent, and Christian population' (1868, 6). The secularist movement, led first by Holyoake and later by Bradlaugh, was increasing its influence among skilled workmen (Simon, 1960, 344), and such men were particularly embittered by what they considered the obstructive wranglings of the churches over who should control the minds of the poor.

It is not surprising that the state turned to the problem with a new sense of urgency, or, in view of past history, that it had only vague and confused notions as to what should and could be done.

4

The Elementary Education
Act, 1870

The League and the Union

The extension of the franchise in 1867 greatly increased the political strength of the Nonconformists, and during the campaign preceding the first general election to be held on the new roll (1868) many Liberal candidates pledged themselves to work for 'equality in religion' and the provision of a national system of elementary education free from 'sectarianism'. The Liberals came to power with a majority of more than 100 seats, and Gladstone became Prime Minister. Though a number of leading Radicals were elected, only one, John Bright, was included in the cabinet, and his activity was negligible because of illness; but another, W. E. Forster, who had earlier been associated with Cobden and Bright in the work of the National Public School Association, became vice-president of the Committee of Council on Education.

The abolition of church-rates by the new government in 1868, and the passing of an act in the following year to disestablish the Church of Ireland, seemed important steps towards a complete separation between the Anglican church and the state; but this made many all the more determined that no new prop for the Church of England should now become available in the form of rate aid for Anglican schools. The danger was obvious, for in 1868-9 about three-quarters of the annual state grant for elementary education in England and Wales (excluding parochial union schools) went to Anglican schools, and the proportion of the total grants since 1839 had been of the same order (see statistics in *M.C.C.*, 1869-70, lxxviii).

The collapse of the Voluntaryist movement increased the tension in three ways: (*a*) it unified and immensely strengthened the ranks of those Nonconformists who were realistically aware of the need for state aid for secular education, yet opposed to such support for religious instruction; (*b*) the former Voluntaryists found themselves in a very disadvantageous position with regard to teacher training for, relying on their own resources, they had been able to build few colleges, and since grants in aid of building had been discontinued by a minute of January 1860 they were now unable to catch up with their rivals and qualify to the same extent for the generous annual support grants currently available; (c) there had been much discouragement and slackening of effort among the Voluntaryists as the impending failure of their policy became obvious, so that the Established Church seemed likely to forge still further ahead in the field of elementary education.

There were naturally many differences of opinion among those who demanded a national system of elementary education based on rate aid for non-denominational schools. To campaign for this the Education Aid Society in Birmingham developed into the National Education League (1869), among its most prominent leaders being George Dixon, an Anglican, as chairman; Dr R. W. Dale, a well-known Congregationalist minister; Dr H. W. Crosskey, a Unitarian minister; and Joseph Chamberlain, a politically ambitious Unitarian and Radical. To represent Nonconformist opinion in particular, and to promote united action, the Central Nonconformist Committee was established in 1870, with its headquarters also in Birmingham: its relations with the League were very close and Dale and Crosskey became its honorary secretaries. Though many Wesleyans favoured continued support for their own denominational schools, a large group within that body had been alienated by the Anglican Church's attitude to the 'conscience clause' (Rigg, 1873, 345) and its continued 'Romanizing' tendencies; there was much opposition to rate support for Anglican schools in single-school areas and for Roman Catholic schools.

It had long been a tradition of the working-class movement to demand education for the workers, and at the second meeting of the newly established Trades Union Congress, held in Birmingham in 1869, a motion was carried unanimously that 'this Congress believes that nothing short of national, unsectarian, and compulsory education will satisfy the requirements of the people of the United Kingdom' (Simon, 1960, 362). The inaugural meeting of the National Education League was addressed by leading trade unionists, and two were elected to the executive: these and others were active in many parts of the country, often through Working Men's Auxiliary Committees (ibid., 363).

The National Education League was extremely well organized and active; it established branch committees in all the important towns in England and gained the adherence of many Nonconformists and liberal Anglicans by conceding that in the proposed rate-aided schools simple Bible reading without note or comment might be permitted if the ratepayers so decided. It was later agreed that even denominational instruction might be given outside school hours, as in the Irish System. A similar association set up in Wales, the Welsh Educational Alliance, attempted to be more firm: it wished to see denominational schools taken over by the local authorities, and religious teaching left to parents and churches; but its demand that education should be both 'secular and unsectarian' (*Hansard*, CXCIX, 1936-7) revealed some confusion and division in its ranks.

Many Denominationalists, in their turn, supported the National Education Union, established to demand support from rates and taxes for denominational schools. So as to prevent further burdens being placed on Denominationalists, it campaigned to oppose the abolition of school fees (except for the children of paupers and vagrants) and to ensure that education should not be made compulsory, unless indirectly through the extension of the Factory Acts. By this time the National Society was very reluctantly disposed to concede a 'conscience clause' for its schools, though there was still opposition from some High Church supporters. The attitude of the Roman Catholic authorities was influenced by their great need of aid and their knowledge that most Protestant parents sufficiently interested to avail themselves of a 'conscience clause' would be unlikely to send children to Roman Catholic schools; but there were considerable misgivings, and Dr Vaughan (the future cardinal) deplored advocacy of the 'conscience clause' as being 'dangerous, and therefore hostile, to the prospects of Christian education' (1868, 32).

'Filling in the gaps'

It may help to clarify the provisions of the Act of 1870 if we consider them in the light of the deficiencies and difficulties discussed earlier: the need for more and better schools almost everywhere; the question of finance (including the desirability of support from local rates), and the problems, especially with regard to control, to which this would give rise; the provision to be made for religious instruction in schools assisted from public funds.

In February 1870 Forster introduced the government's Bill 'to provide for public elementary education in England and Wales'. He claimed that only two-fifths of the children of the working classes between the ages of six and ten years were on the registers of the state-aided schools, and only one-third of those between the ages of ten and twelve (actual attendance was much lower); the schools which did not receive government assistance were, generally speaking, 'the worst schools, and those least fitted to give a good education to the children of the working classes'. In Manchester and Liverpool a quarter of such children were not attending school and many others were receiving an education 'not worth having'. Forster went on: 'The result of the State leaving the initiative to volunteers, is that where State help has been most wanted, State help has been least given, and that where it was desirable that State power should be most felt it was not felt at all' (*Hansard*, CXCIX, 441-3).

Forster announced the government's intention to ensure the provision 'throughout the kingdom' of 'sufficient, efficient and suitable' elementary schools (ibid., CXCIX, 445). But the state would take care 'not to destroy the existing system in building a new one'; it would not 'neglect voluntary help', but would 'welcome it'. Nor was this solely to avoid enormous extra expense. Gladstone praised the denominational system as evincing 'the spirit of Christianity working in the minds of men'; moreover, he considered it 'desirable never to multiply the establishments of the Government beyond what is necessary, but, where it is possible, to avail ourselves of private energy and zeal' (ibid., CCIII, 747).

Accordingly, the aim of the government, Forster announced, would be 'to complete the present voluntary system, to fill up the gaps, sparing the public money where it can be done without ... and welcoming as much as we rightly can the co-operation and aid of those benevolent men who desire to assist their neighbours' (ibid., CXCIX, 443-4). Therefore, when the state had ascertained in every part of England and Wales what facilities for elementary education, whether public or private, already existed, the voluntary bodies would be allowed a period of grace, 'not exceeding six months', to present plans for making good the deficiencies with the help of the existing state building grants. After the completion of the schools whose plans were approved, such grants would cease to be made.

Originally the government had proposed a period of grace of twelve months, and had had to reduce this in the face of hostile criticism: in practice it lasted until the last day of 1870, less than five months after the Bill became law. The provision constituted a concession, a challenge and, in effect, a pledge. As a concession it was much greater than it seemed, for it was an invitation to the voluntary bodies to make as many proposals as they wished, without the restraint involved in accepting firm commitments; far more than the normal number of plans were of course submitted during the statutory period, and though about one in nine of these was rejected and two out of five withdrawn the last building grant was not made until 1881 (*R.C.C.*, 1881-2, xl). The invitation to the voluntary bodies, and its results, showed beyond reasonable argument that, even with their most strenuous endeavours and this new encouragement to demonstrate their powers, they could not provide an adequate system of elementary education under existing financial arrangements. Yet they had now been invited to make an exceptional effort and to spend considerable sums on building new schools: in the eleven years ending in December 1881 state building grants in respect of such schools in England and Wales were met by 'local contributions' more than four times as great (ibid.). Not surprisingly, Denominationalists felt entitled to expect the continuance of state support.

Financial provisions of the Act

Forster put forward the familiar arguments in favour of state intervention: the need to reduce crime and misery, to improve the supply of skilled labour so as to meet competition from abroad, and to fit the new voters for their responsibilities. But too much direct state provision and control of education he considered undesirable: no 'central department' could cope with the task, and, if it could, 'enormous power' would be given to the central administration. There must therefore be reliance on 'local agency', and, since 'voluntary local agency' had failed, the state would seek 'the help of municipal organization', this involving support 'by means of rates aided by money voted by Parliament, expended under local management, with central inspection and control' (*Hansard*, CXCIX, 451). The government had to withdraw its original proposal that the school boards established for this purpose should be elected by town councils in boroughs and vestries in parishes. Instead, in response to the demands of Nonconformists and Radicals, it had to concede direct voting by ratepayers, and even, after most heated debates, voting by ballot – though this provision was abandoned when rejected by the Lords, and retained only for elections in London.

The government at first proposed, in Forster's words, that the school boards 'may either provide schools themselves, or assist the present schools, or they may do both. But there is this condition, that if they do go on the principle of assisting, they must assist all schools on equal terms. They may not pick out one particular denomination and say – "We shall assist you, but not the others" ' (ibid., CXCIX, 456).

Two principles were involved here: whether denominational schools should receive rate aid at all, and whether the decision on this should be left to local school boards or taken for the whole country by the state. With regard to the second, critics claimed that the government was 'shirking the difficulty, not settling it'; that 'the point ought to be determined by Parliament, and not feebly left to be fought over every year in every parish'; and that 'the provision that if one school is aided, all must be, is a farce; for in rural parishes there is only one school, and if there are more there ought not to be' (ibid., CXCIX, 1972, 1973). On the other hand, the Denominationalists would have been at the mercy of some hostile school boards. Manchester Town Council and some of the London vestries indicated their reluctance 'to take upon themselves the unfettered discretion of dealing with the religious question' (ibid., CCII, 1249).

But still more influential was the extremely bitter criticism of the whole principle of spending rates on denominational schools. Of the two chief objections, so often repeated in the past and the future, one was expressed by the Radical Nonconformist member for Merthyr Tydfil, who claimed it to be one of the most fundamental and universally recognized principles of Nonconformity

that it was not right to take money received from the general taxation of the country and apply it to purposes of religious instruction and worship ... if they claimed the right to compel one man to pay for the support of another man's religion, and to enforce that, as they must, by penalties of law, they passed at once into the region of religious persecution (ibid., CCII, 498-9).

The second was voiced even more pointedly by R. W. Dale: 'We respect Mr Forster – we honour Mr Gladstone; but we are determined that England shall not again be cursed with the bitterness and strife from which we hoped we had for ever escaped by the abolition of the Church rate' (Dale, A. W. W., 1899, 275).

The government withdrew the proposal that denominational schools might receive rate aid, and thereby evaded having to decide what local control might be demanded in return; but, as the result of an oversight typical of much of the slipshod drafting and handling of the Bill, a clause was allowed to stand empowering school boards to use rates in order to reduce or pay the fees of individual necessitous children attending *all* the public elementary schools within its area, including denominational schools: this of course involved the hated principle of rate support and gave rise to unmeasured controversy later.

There was to be no question of the state's making education compulsory (though school boards were given powers to do so) or of providing instruction free, except for very necessitous children. The cost of dispensing with school pence, it was considered, would be 'enormous'; working-class parents must be kept aware of their responsibilities; there was also a danger that middle-class parents might come to demand free education for their children. Hitherto the state grant had been payable 'to promote the education of children belonging to the classes who support themselves by manual labour' : now it would be made available where the school fee did not exceed ninepence a week – a surprisingly high maximum, more than sufficient in itself to cover the average annual expenditure per child in existing state-aided schools. This raised an issue highly important to those opposed to state support for denominational schools : the church authorities justified their claim to teach their own creeds by pointing to their contributions to the schools, but what if the schools were maintained wholly from public funds and payments from parents (who were widely believed to care little about denominational distinctions)? Gladstone accepted the point and gave a firm undertaking :

> We shall take care that, under no circumstances, shall the public grants be allowed so to operate as to supply, together with school pence, the sum necessary to support these schools, and that there shall always remain a void which must be filled up by voluntary contributions, and without which, failing other sources of assistance, these schools would no longer deserve the character of voluntary (*Hansard*, CCII, 938).

Yet less than three weeks later Forster was praising in the House elementary schools maintained only by state grants and high fees; he asked, as if Gladstone had never spoken on this important principle of state policy, 'Were the government to say that those schools were not to have any grant because the parents were prepared to pay more than parents usually did pay and there were no voluntary subscriptions?' (ibid., CCIII, 88). No reference was made in the act to Gladstone's undertaking; and Forster rejected a proposal that children of better-off parents might be excluded from elementary schools, observing that 'in many cases there might be considerable advantage in having children of all classes attending the same school' (ibid., CCII, 1265).

One curious feature of the financial provisions of the Act was the formal statement in it that with regard to state assistance there would be no 'preference or advantage to any school on the ground that it is or is not provided by a school board'. True, there was a proviso permitting additional grant to school boards where a 3d. rate did not provide a stated sum considered to be adequate, but Gladstone was convinced that this would never arise, and he would have preferred 'to dispense altogether with this contingent reserve of liability from the Exchequer' (ibid., CCII, 280). The function of the state would be to adopt a neutral rôle, giving assistance on equal terms to board and voluntary schools, both of them relying for the rest of their income on fees and what (to emphasize the parallelism) was referred to in official minutes as 'local exertion' – i.e., rates in the case of board schools, voluntary contributions in other cases. Thus fair competition would be established. But this equating of rates and voluntary subscriptions was, of course, ludicrous, since rates manifestly were a more reliable and readily expansible source of income, subscriptions were likely to fall when they appeared less necessary, and, in any case, voluntary contributors had also to pay rates. Indeed rates were even levied on the voluntary schools themselves.

The amount of state grant was not prescribed in the Act, but Gladstone undertook to increase it in order to compensate for the withdrawal of building grants. He claimed that the average cost for each child attending a state-aided elementary school was annually about 30s. od., provided in roughly equal amounts from fees, voluntary contributions and an *average* state grant earned (largely as 'payment by results') of about 10s. od. (*Hansard*, CCII, 280). To meet the new situation, the state grant to voluntary (and hence board) schools would be raised so that the *maximum* which could be earned would be 15s. od. (*if equalled by other income*). This was considered to be a rise of 50 per cent. But this revealed utter arithmetical confusion, for the existing maximum, rarely earned, was already 15s. od., and of course what mattered was raising the *average* grant actually obtained. By 1873 the average state grant paid had in fact risen from about 10s. od. to only about 12s. od.: it did not rise to 15s. od. for Church of England schools until 1881 (Rigg, 1873, 365-6). Moreover, by insisting that the amount of state grant would depend on 'results' (an obvious hardship for the poorer and less efficient schools), and that however much was thus 'earned' no more would be paid than was provided by 'local exertion' and fees, the state not only gave a great advantage to board schools but perpetuated the very principle which Forster had forcibly denounced in his opening speech: 'that where State help has been most wanted, State help has been least given'.

The problem of religious instruction

There is no doubt that some of the anomalies of the Act of 1870 received scant notice because so much excited attention was directed to discussion of the 'religious difficulty'. To some extent the issues were as they long had been, but in fact some long-defended positions had now been surrendered, in particular the claim of the Established Church for more favourable treatment, the 'conscience clause' and the contentions that state assistance for education could be dispensed with, or should be given without requiring some degree of control. It even appeared unsurprising that Gladstone, his youthful notions about church and state far behind him, should now insist on the secular rôle of the modern state.

For the government now declared that henceforth it would be providing funds only in aid of secular education; so far from insisting, as in the past, that government assistance would be given only to support schools which provided religious instruction, the state formally declared in the Act that no grant would be made 'in respect of any instruction in religious subjects', and that there would be no requirement 'that the school shall be in connexion with a religious denomination, or that religious instruction shall be given in the school'. Individual state inspectors would not be assigned to particular denominations to accord with the latter's doctrinal predilections, religious instruction in Church of England schools would no longer be examined by the inspectors, and therefore payment of grant to them would cease to be dependent on the efficiency of the religious teaching: it was specifically pointed out that the existing practice was 'unfair' to other denominations and therefore inconsistent with the state's new rôle. Kay-Shuttleworth, Forster remarked, had 'established – concordats with the different denominations ... because he found it almost impossible to help it' (*Hansard*, CXCIX, 447). Now, he clearly implied, times had changed, and for the better.

The 'secular' principle was further emphasized in relation to the 'conscience clause': this would apply not merely to new schools in single-school areas, as had recently become the practice; henceforth the right of withdrawal from religious instruction must be allowed in all schools receiving grants from public funds. The government's initial proposal was that permission for withdrawal must be requested in writing – clearly a serious hindrance for many parents; in the face of criticism not only was this stipulation abandoned but the state accepted a new provision – that, to facilitate withdrawal from religious instruction, this might be given only at the beginning or end (or both) of a school meeting. His continued insistence that secular and religious instruction not only could, but must, be separated was the key-note of the state's new policy; its reluctant acceptance by the Denominationalists implied the abandonment of their former demand for a wholly denominational 'atmosphere' in their schools.

But what of religious instruction in the board schools? Gladstone himself was quite prepared to forbid such instruction altogether, leaving it to be given, where it was desired, outside school hours, at the ratepayers' expense or otherwise, by the school teachers or others, on or off the school premises. He wrote: 'We might have fallen back upon the plan of confining the rate to secular subjects;

but this was opposed by the church, the opposition, most of the dissenters, and most of our own friends' (Morley, 1903, II, 306).

We have seen that the National Education League and the Welsh Educational Alliance had been obliged, for the sake of preserving unity and winning maximum support, to favour 'unsectarian' religious instruction, but it was difficult to arrive at an acceptable version of this, and vague references to 'those general truths on which all Christians agree' were not helpful. Our own ideas of what constitutes 'undenominational religion' are coloured by modern agreements arrived at in practice mainly by orthodox Protestants. But the definition given by George Dixon, the chairman and chief parliamentary spokesman of the League, was much more narrow:

> The difference between an unsectarian and a secular system appeared to be this – that in both you would exclude all Christian dogmas, but in an unsectarian ... system you would not have to exclude Christian precepts. As to those awkward questions which exceptional children might put to a master asking the authority for such precepts, if in the answer were involved the acknowledgment of a future state of existence or of a God, he still thought that would be unsectarian teaching (Hansard, CXCIX, 1923-4).

There were also broader interpretations, of course, but that Dixon's was shared by others is shown by Cardinal Manning's plea in 1888 that undenominational teaching should not preclude references to God.

In March, 1870, Gladstone wrote to Earl Russell:

> Men are decided [sic] not between two courses or even three, but four or five: secularism, Bible-reading only, Bible-reading with unsectarian teaching (to be limited and defined on appeal by a new sort of Pope in the Council Office), Bible reading with unlimited exposition, or, lastly, this plus Catechism and formularies (Correspondence, ed. Lathbury, II, 138).

The government eventually decided in favour of the first and fourth of these, and after prolonged and angry discussion its proposals were carried. School boards, if they wished, might exclude all religious instruction from their schools. An amendment proposing to make compulsory 'the daily reading and teaching of the Bible' was rejected by the resounding majority of 250 to eighty-one. On the other hand it was laid down, in the terms of a motion proposed by Mr Cowper-Temple, that where religious instruction was given 'no religious catechism or religious formulary which is distinctive of any particular denomination' should be taught.

It has not generally been appreciated that this 'Cowper-Temple clause' was intended only to prohibit the use of catechisms and similar formulations of faith, not to forbid the expression of the teacher's own doctrinal beliefs. This was well understood by the government's critics, one of whom pointed out that the objections to Denominationalism were not met by an amendment 'merely forbidding the teaching of one or two well-known and recognised formularies' (*Hansard*, CCII, 844). Forster explained that the government had accepted the Cowper-Temple amendment chiefly because 'there was an objection in the country to catechisms and special formularies ... not so much on account of the actual words, but because the putting of them into the hands of children appeared to be like claiming those children as belonging to a particular Church'. He recognized that 'it was quite true that you may have sectarian teaching without sectarian formularies and catechisms' (ibid., CCII, 1251, 590). Cowper-Temple himself rejected any proposal 'that measures should be taken to deprive the teachers in the schools created under the Bill, of the right, which everybody else in this country enjoyed, to explain the Bible according to his own views and opinions' (ibid., CCIII, 739). He considered that 'the exclusion of catechisms and formularies left the opinions and faith of the teacher untouched, and dealt only with lesson books which bore upon their title-page plain indications of their origin' (ibid., CCII, 1277).

When Forster told the Commons that the government 'had to take into consideration the clearly expressed desire of the country for what was called unsectarian education', the Prime Minister hastened to remove any misapprehension about the government's position:

> My right hon. friend ... has said that the Government sympathised with the desire for unsectarian teaching in schools, and I am prepared to support that statement in what I conceive to be its true sense – namely, it is our wish that the exposition of the Bible in schools should take its natural course; that it should be confined to the simple and devout method of handling which is adapted to the understanding and characters of children; but we do not admit that the simple and devout character of teaching can be secured by an attempt to exclude all reference to tenets and doctrines. That is an exclusion which cannot be effected, and, if it could, it ought not to be; it is an invasion of the freedom of religious teaching such as ought not to be tolerated in this country (ibid., CCII, 1256).

Gladstone explicitly declared later that there must be 'free exposition of the Scriptures open to every schoolmaster who may be conscientiously attached to the Nonconformist community, subject, of course, as I hope he will be, to the restraints of common-sense, but to no other restraints of a legal kind' (ibid., CCIII, 748).

The disputants were left in no doubt about government policy when a vote was taken on an amendment, proposed by Jacob Bright, providing that 'In any [board] school in which the Bible shall be read and taught the teaching shall not be used or directed in favour of or against the distinctive tenets of any religious denomination' (ibid., CCII, 1271). The crucial proposal was opposed by the government and the Conservatives and was overwhelmingly rejected; but of 376 Liberals present only 121 voted with the government – 132 voted against it and 133 abstained. There was deep resentment that denominational teaching in board schools was to be sanctioned only as a consequence of Conservative support.

Gladstone, who later claimed that he had 'never made greater personal concessions of opinion than on the Education Bill' (Morley, 1903, II, 298), was nevertheless adamant on this point. After the Bill had passed he wrote, 'I assure you, the very utmost that could be done was to arrange the matter as it now stands, where the exclusion is limited to the formulary, and to get rid of the popular imposture of undenominational religion' (Morley, 1903, II, 306). The state had stumbled upon a policy which seemed manifestly unworkable, but it had at least the inestimable merit of obtaining a majority in the Commons and even proving acceptable in the Lords. It is surely one of the oddities of history that, after decades of discussion and strife, this 'solution' to part of the 'religious difficulty' was at last agreed upon by the state and the denominational authorities, thus making vast progress possible – yet, as we shall see, it was promptly ignored nearly everywhere and soon almost entirely forgotten.

Reactions of Denominationalists and their opponents

Though the Anglicans had fought hard against parts of the Act, they had entered the contest with considerable apprehension because of the extension of the franchise, their need for financial aid and, above all, the well organized opposition of the National Education League: most were therefore relieved that greater concessions had not been demanded of them. The feelings of many were summed up by that old die-hard defender of the Church of England, the Earl of Shaftesbury (formerly Lord Ashley) who thought that

the government had saved a great deal for the friends of scriptural education ... he felt as sure as he did of anything that if this Bill were lost a measure of purely secular education would be passed by the House of Commons next year. He believed that even many of those who had stood up for the Bill this year would in another give up the struggle from mere weariness (*Hansard*, CCIII, 1168).

Many of the Roman Catholic clergy (in particular Dr Ullathorne, Bishop of Birmingham) and some of the laity were extremely critical of the Bill, but though 'the Catholic Poor School Committee petitioned the Commons, and interviewed the Catholic M.P.'s and the Government four times' (Beales, 1950, 374), there was little effective opposition. At the material times all but one of the bishops were attending the Vatican Council, and 'the first personal contact between the Bishops and the Poor School Committee occurred on the day the Bill received the Royal Assent' (ibid., 374; McClelland, 77). Gladstone informed Manning that 'communications with those who represented his Communion' had appeared to indicate that they could not accept rate aid on the state's terms: the secretary of the Catholic Poor School Committee had told Gladstone that if the government paid half of the 'school charges' the Committee 'could perhaps perform their work', and this, Gladstone thought, would 'now be secured for efficient schools by the proposals of the Government' (*Correspondence*, ed. Lathbury, II, 1910, 140).

Manning himself asked Gladstone for rate aid payable by the decision of the government, not at the discretion of a local board, as had first been proposed. He could see no reason why rate support could not be made available on terms similar to those of the Reformatory and Industrial School Acts. Once assured of freedom from local control he adopted the policy of seeking Roman Catholic membership of school boards so as to minimize the danger of their hostility and 'to obtain a share in the treatment of questions which may affect us' (McClelland, 1962, 70, 71). In the House of Lords, Lord Howard of Glossop, president of the Catholic Poor School Committee, complained that the board schools could not provide the religious atmosphere which Roman Catholics sought for their children, and he observed that the boards would have the advantages of superior resources and the power to remit fees. Nevertheless he acknowledged that the Bill was 'a measure which required skill and boldness to bring forward' at a time when there was so much hostility to voluntary schools, and he 'hoped it would pass into law' (*Hansard*, CCIII, 852).

One of the most notable immediate results of the passing of the Elementary Education Act of 1870 was to antagonize many of those Nonconformists, Secularists and liberal churchmen who had hitherto supported the Liberals. The government was accused of having 'trampled on some of the most deeply-cherished convictions of half the people in the land' (*Hansard*, CXCIX, 1971); Edward Miall claimed that 'there was scarcely a dissenting organisation in

the country that had not pronounced condemnation' of the Bill;
the Nonconformists, 'the heart, and, he might say, the hands of
the Liberal cause', had been the main force bringing the Liberal
party to power, but now, 'once bit, twice shy' (ibid., CCIII, 742,
743).

Some results of the Act

Some of the consequences of the passing of the Act we have already
noted: the firm establishment at long last of a national framework
for elementary education in England and Wales; the setting up of
the 'dual system' and the virtual pledge of its continuance; the
acceptance by the state of its 'secular rôle', of the need to treat all
sects alike, and of the desirability of neutrality in its relations
with school boards and Denominationalists (though in practice, as
we shall see, the Liberals and Radicals much favoured the former
and the Conservatives the latter). The Anglicans and Roman Catholics were drawn together, not by formal agreements but by
community of interest, and this to the great advantage of both,
since the Roman Catholic Church benefited from the great political
influence of the Established Church and in turn lent added credi-
bility to the contention that conscientious issues and parental
wishes were indeed at stake.

The Act greatly increased the control of the central government
over elementary education, though the arguments in favour of
establishing a Ministry or Board of Education, put forward by Earl
Russell, George Dixon and others, went unheeded. Not only was
the system of 'payment by results', with its prescribed syllabuses
and detailed inspection, to remain in being: the Education Department was now to decide where new schools were needed, where
school boards should be set up, which of their bye-laws might be
approved, and what fees might be charged in board schools. If
the Department considered a board to be in default it was
empowered to constitute a new board merely by nominating its
members. Lay control of elementary education was vastly increased;
no longer could church leaders hold up the establishment of
schools (or threaten to do so) unless their conditions were met;
and though many of the clergy became members of school boards
there were relatively few in which their word was law.

The result was a rise in the status of the teachers, since so many
were now to be freed from clerical control and doctrinal tests. It
was not that sudden changes were likely, since most of the training
colleges were controlled by denominational bodies and the Act
did nothing to change this, though state grants of up to 75 per cent
were now payable: indeed governors of such colleges were ex-

pressly empowered by the Committee of Council to select students 'on their own responsibility, subject to no other conditions on the part of the Education Department' than those relating to age and suitability (*M.C.C.*, 1870-1, cxvi). Moreover those appointing teachers to board schools were often deeply concerned about religion. Nevertheless, in the long run, given the absence of close clerical control and selection, teachers in board schools could react more readily to changes in the climate of opinion in society as a whole. But other more immediate developments were important. The views of teachers on the Bill of 1870 were sought in various parts of the country; there was general agreement among them that the 'religious problem' was 'only a "platform difficulty" ' and of little concern to parents, whilst a 'conscience clause' was workable. A significant reaction was the feeling that to restrict instruction to purely secular subjects would 'degrade the teachers in the eyes of the public' (Tropp, 1957, 105). Lord Brougham had hoped in 1820 that the teacher would become 'a lay parson' (*Hansard*, II, 74), but mounting widespread apprehension among the clergy had been expressed by the Roman Catholic Bishop Ullathorne: 'Schoolmasters are already beginning to fancy themselves wiser in their spheres than clergymen' (1857, 63). The consultations over the 1870 Bill gave many teachers a greater awareness of their powers and common purposes, and encouraged them to set up the National Union of Elementary Teachers, able to speak with greater authority than the denominational unions hitherto existing. At its first conference its president 'claimed that in the voluntary schools, teachers had been forced to become religious partisans. The Education Act of 1870 had given the teacher a measure of freedom and independence' (Tropp, 1957, 110).

Of course many teachers willingly remained 'partisans', but the freedom not to be so became a mark of professional pride, and this was important for the working of the Act. Equally important in the future was the conviction, already referred to, that responsibility for religious instruction raised the teacher's standing: this sentiment was constantly repeated (e.g. Fitch, 1894, 66, and the Reservation to the *Final Report* of the Cross Commission, 1888, 393, made by T. E. Heller, general secretary of the N.U.E.T.). The three factors: the growing organized strength of the teachers in a sphere where their co-operation was essential; the unwillingness of many of them to act as religious 'partisans' as a condition of employment; and their reluctance to hand over religious instruction to the clergy or others, became important new factors in the situation.

The position in Ireland and in Scotland

Many who had fought hard to change the provisions of the Act scorned the government's assurance that the country would not be committed to 'any definite scheme': they predicted that henceforward England and Wales would be unalterably committed to Denominationalism (*Hansard*, CCII, 844). Ireland, too, would be involved. For a generation those in England and Wales who were opposed to the denominational system had hoped that the 'Irish System' would eventually provide a model for a 'united' and undenominational policy at home, but the failure of Russell's attempt to introduce the system in 1839, and the consequent payment of state grants since 1847 to Roman Catholic schools, had weakened the support for its continuance in Ireland. The Presbyterians in the north, and the Roman Catholic Archbishop McHale and his followers in the south, had long campaigned for unrestricted liberty to give denominational instruction in the national schools; the mounting hostility of the Roman Catholic authorities to 'united education' had been shown in their opposition to plans for undenominational universities and training colleges. The more active Nonconformists and Radicals in England made the preservation of the 'Irish National System' one of the objects of the National Education League, but the system had already been undermined in practice by 1870, and the Act helped further to destroy it. In 1883, as a modern Irish historian has put it, the Irish Board of National Education 'gave way, and henceforth the policy of Archbishop McHale triumphed. A deep gulf was fixed between the Roman Catholic and Protestant National Schools until they almost seemed instead of a stone's throw to be centuries apart' (Auchmuty, 1937, 149).

In Scotland, on the other hand, the denominational system was so firmly established that there was little possibility of change. The Education (Scotland) Act of 1872 went further than the 1870 Act by providing for the establishment of school boards throughout the country, but there was not, as in England and Wales, any limitation of the kind of religious instruction to be given (beyond requiring the right of withdrawal). Almost all the school boards in fact prescribed continuance of the form of religious instruction hitherto given, i.e. Presbyterian. Most of those in charge of voluntary schools were prepared to accept this arrangement and transferred the properties to the boards; those who could not (chiefly those who belonged to the Roman Catholic or Scottish Episcopalian churches, or who favoured undenominational religious instruction) provided their own schools and received state grants, but not rate support.

5

The Act in operation

The school boards

When Forster was reproached with having failed to bring forward a measure likely to endure for at least twenty years, he replied that he would be content even if modifications became necessary 'within two or three years' (*Hansard*, CCIII, 759). The League, the Central Nonconformist Committee and the Union stayed in being to continue the struggle, it being generally felt that since the state had failed to produce an acceptable settlement, the final outcome would depend largely on the interpretation and working of the Act.

In 1872 the League came out in favour of the compulsory establishment of school boards in all districts, existing denominational schools to fall under the control of school boards for secular instruction, with such religious instruction as Denominationalists desired being provided by them outside school hours at their own expense. The Central Nonconformist Committee, at a meeting presided over by Joseph Chamberlain, announced that for the future its aims, *inter alia*, would be to secure the amendment of those provisions of the Act which 'violated the principles of religious liberty', to ensure the refusal of state grants to new denominational schools, and to bring about the gradual withdrawal of such grants from 'schools under sectarian management' (Adams, 1882, 239).

Most of the smaller Methodist bodies shared these ideas, and, for reasons given earlier, the official policy of the Wesleyans now hardened further against that of the Anglicans and Roman Catholics. In 1872 a special committee appointed by the Wesleyan Methodist Conference 'while resolving to maintain in full vigour and efficiency' their 'connexial day schools and training colleges', was of the opinion that, 'due regard being had to existing interests, future legislation for primary education at the public cost should provide for such education only on the principle of unsectarian schools under the school board'. The Conference endorsed this resolution and called upon the state to establish school boards everywhere, and place 'an undenominational school within reasonable distance of every family' (quoted C.C., III, 51).

Naturally the Denominationalist Union sought to limit the number of board schools, as being unsatisfactory on religious grounds and likely to become unfair rivals. Great efforts and sacrifices were made by the Denominationalists to build schools, and they were helped by some individuals and organizations moved not so much by zeal for education as by the desire to avoid paying increased rates to a school board (C.C., *Final Report*, 1883, 369). In Stockport the Denominationalists who controlled the board even brought about its abolition in 1879 as being unnecessary, though existing schools were sufficient only because relatively high fees were charged and a large number of Protestant children were accommodated in Roman Catholic schools (ibid., 266).

In many areas, especially in rural districts, either there was no need for board schools, or the boards were almost exclusively controlled by Anglicans. But in many others, and especially in the larger towns, the struggle to obtain places on the boards and decide their policies became merely an extension of the old conflict by new means. It would, of course, be wrong to suggest that Denominational members of boards were universally indifferent to educational considerations. It seemed natural to many Nonconformists that in board schools standards of equipment, accommodation and teaching should be as high as was practicable and not kept down to those of voluntary schools whose supporters, whilst seeking adherents to their religion, were unwilling or unable to give them adequate support it seemed equally justifiable to Denominationalists to prevent unfair competition and an increase in rates, which they had themselves to pay in addition to their school subscriptions. It is also understandable that good reasons were easily found for intolerant and bigoted conduct on both sides. The situation could hardly be described as promising.

The 'new type of Pope in the Council Office'

Though the state had sought to avoid responsibility for all but secular education it was nevertheless the custodian of an Act of Parliament which virtually made it necessary, in spite of Gladstone, to have 'a new type of Pope in the Council Office', ready to give rulings concerning religious instruction. A single example may be of interest. As soon as the Act was passed, Forster sought such a ruling from the Prime Minister himself, and was advised that the Apostle's Creed was not a 'distinctive formulary' and therefore could be taught in board schools. In 1886 the Secretary to the Education Department informed Cardinal Manning that there was 'no certainty about the matter' (C.C., *First Report*, 25). Two years later the teaching of the Creed was formally sanctioned (*R.R.T.*, 1888, 400). But the decision of the state was widely ignored. One former inspector considered (1894) that the Apostle's Creed was regarded by most Nonconformists as 'virtually an Anglican formulary' and its use in a board school as 'contrary to the whole spirit and intention of Mr Forster's Act' (Fitch, 1894, 61-2). He claimed that even the dominant 'dogmatic' (i.e. Denominationalist) group on the London board did not venture to advocate its inclusion in the religious syllabus, and a leader of that group, Canon Gregory, complained in 1895 that its teaching was prohibited 'by most School Boards' (1905, 130).

As far as possible the Education Department avoided trouble by pleading inability to act in the absence of complaints from parents (these being rare) but sometimes decisions had to be taken. Thus, after protests from the militant Protestant Alliance in 1872, Cardinal Manning was persuaded to withdraw from use in Roman Catholic schools during ordinary lesson time readers which contained doctrinal teaching and unfavourable references to the Reformation (McClelland, 1964, 175). In 1888, thirty-four rural board schools admitted using the Anglican Catechism, and when nine seemed slow to mend their ways, the Education Department warned them that recognition would be withdrawn (implying loss of grant) 'if any part of the Church Catechism except the Lord's Prayer, Ten Commandments, and the Apostle's Creed is taught in a Board school during school hours'; the offending boards were asked to 'pass and communicate to the Department some formal regulation in conformity with the above direction' (*R.R.T.*, 1888, 400).

The boards and the Cowper-Temple Clause

Yet as soon as the Act was passed it became clear that in general it was not the state but the school boards and the teachers who would effectively decide what religious instruction would be given in board schools. It would have been impracticable in any case to leave every teacher free to teach his particular beliefs (one can only suppose that Gladstone was assuming that Roman Catholics or Unitarians would not teach in such schools). Minorities were usually represented on school boards, thanks to the system of voting, which allowed each voter as many votes as there were places on the school board but allowed him to give them all to one candidate or spread them over a few if he so desired: the result in most places was a gradual move towards establishing some consensus of opinion. However heated electoral campaigns and boardroom debates might become, urgent practical decisions had now to be taken, and most of the boards, including many controlled by Denominationalists, quite quickly opted for undenominational teaching of one kind or another, explicitly going beyond the Cowper-Temple clause. Thus the Sheffield board instructed its teachers

> not only to adhere strictly to the terms of the 14th Section of the Education Act, which provides that no 'religious formulary which is distinctive of any religious denomination shall be taught in the school', but also to abstain from all denominational teaching (Bingham, 1949, 159).

In Leicester the Liberals proposed that the Bible be read without note or comment, and, when this move failed, suggested equally unsuccessfully that it be read without reference to God. It was finally agreed that when explanations of the Bible were given no attempt should be made to attach children to, nor detach them from, any particular denomination – this being an echo of the Jacob Bright amendment which Parliament in 1870 had specifically rejected. For greater safety only narrative sections of the Bible might be read (Simon, 1968, 167). In London, though a few members of the first board favoured Bible reading without note or comment, whilst some Nonconformists objected to any religious instruction at all being given in rate-supported schools, the proposal was carried, by a majority of thirty-eight votes to three,

> That in the schools provided by the Board the Bible shall be read, and there shall be given such explanations therefrom in the principles of morality and religion as are suited to the capacities of children, provided ... that in such explanations and instruction the provisions of the Act relating to the 'conscience clause' and the Cowper-Temple clause be strictly observed, both in letter and spirit, and that no attempt be made to attach children to any denomination (Spalding, 1900, 99).

This regulation was copied, sometimes word for word, in many parts of the country, though the Liverpool board eventually added a provision

> That the authorised version of the Bible be used; but that when the Roman Catholic children in the school are sufficiently numerous to form a class, they shall receive instruction from the Douai version of the Bible (*R.R.T.*, 1888, 363, 359).

The adoption by school boards of bye-laws prohibiting denominational instruction became so widespread that more than one member of a Royal Commission was quite astonished in 1886 to be told of the actual legal position, when Mr Cumin, the secretary and legal adviser of the Education Department, explained that denominational instruction could indeed be given in board schools as in voluntary schools, the difference being merely that in the former 'you must not use a catechism or a formulary' (C.C., *First Report*, 24). One man who certainly remembered and understood what parliament had decided in 1870 was the Anglican clergyman, the Rev. J. Nunn, who was chairman of the Manchester School Board in 1887. When asked by the Cross Commission whether his board had adopted 'the usual byelaw that the teaching shall not be in favour of or against the religious tenets of any denomination', he replied:

> Certainly not.... There is nothing to prevent a church teacher in our board schools teaching according to his conscience. That was the intention of the Act of Parliament. It was distinctly refused in the House of Commons to fetter the teachers, and we regard the fettering of the teachers as contrary to the intention of the Act.

To the obvious question which at once occurred to his interrogators he replied with disarming frankness: 'A Catholic would not be allowed as a teacher at a board school because of his religious belief' (C.C., *Second Report*, 1887, 785, 786). In some other areas where Anglicans controlled the school boards, and were aware of their rights under the Act, syllabuses of religious instruction similar to that adopted in Manchester were prescribed; this must have been small consolation in old age to two prime ministers who remembered what had actually been decided in 1870: Lord Salisbury (Gregory, 1905, 129), and Gladstone, who in 1894 still maintained that any undenominational system of religion, framed by the state, was a 'moral monster' and that the provisions of an Act requiring or permitting it would be 'a gross error' (*Correspondence*, ed. Lathbury, 1910, II, 148).

Very few boards took advantage of their legal right to exclude all religious instruction from their schools, though in many it was exiguous. Some who reported that no religious instruction was given added that the Bible was read without comment. A report published in 1888 stated that 'out of 2,225 School Boards ... only 7 in England and 50 in Wales ... have dispensed entirely with Religious Teaching or Observances'; another report in the same year listed twenty-one in England (all in small country areas) and seventy in Wales (C.C., *Final Report*, 113; R.R.T., 408). Of course the relatively high figure for Wales reflected the high proportion of Nonconformists who considered that religious instruction should be left to the minister, the Sunday school and the parents.

In Birmingham, the home of the National Education League and of the Central Nonconformist Committee, Radicals, Liberals and Nonconformists were particularly strong, but because of unskilful use of the novel electoral procedure they did not obtain control of the local school board until 1873: in the meantime Joseph Chamberlain enjoyed demonstrating to candidates for teaching posts that undenominational teaching, which the board prescribed, was quite impossible (Taylor, 1960, 195). By 1872 the League had at last decided to campaign for purely secular teaching, and under the inspiration of R. W. Dale and Chamberlain, the new Birmingham School Board inaugurated the system in 1873, permitting religious instruction to be given only outside school hours, by clergymen or others who were not concerned with the secular instruction, and who even paid to use the classrooms. The policy, for decades advocated as the only logical solution to the religious difficulty, failed, partly because of objections by some Nonconformists, especially Wesleyans, to the exclusion of the Bible from the schools, and partly because of the refusal of Anglicans to cooperate, the incompetence of unpractised instructors and so on (ibid.). From 1879 Bible reading by the head teacher, without note or comment, was permitted. The failure of the 'secular experiment' in Birmingham was taken to be extremely significant and was long remembered. Henceforward the 'secular solution' was advocated chiefly by Socialist and working-class movements (Simon, 1965, 142-155), but an alliance between earnest Nonconformists, those merely repelled by the quarrels of the churches and those who considered religion to be the 'opium of the people' was an uneasy and ineffective one.

Progress towards agreement

The resentment felt by many Nonconformists and Radicals at being, as they claimed, 'betrayed' by a Liberal government, was intense. In the general election of 1874, of the 425 Liberal candidates 300 were pledged to vote for the repeal of the clause in the 1870 Act which empowered school boards to pay from the rates the fees of indigent children attending denominational schools (Morley, 1903, II, 311). School boards had reacted to the clause in accordance with the views of the dominant groups within them. Thus the Manchester board, controlled by Denominationalists, paid fees for many children to attend denominational schools; whilst the Birmingham board was similarly constituted during its first three years of office it wished to do the same, but the Radicals prevented this even before they assumed control of the board, since they used their majority in the town council to bar the levying of the necessary rate. After six years of most acrimonious dispute the

Conservatives in parliament (who had defeated the disrupted Liberals in 1874) transferred the powers in question to the Poor Law Guardians.

In 1886 a Conservative government set up the Cross Commission 'to inquire into the working of the Elementary Education Acts, England and Wales': it spent much time considering complaints from Denominationalists and their opponents, and predictably produced two reports, one supported by the majority, who favoured denominational education, and another signed by those who did not. It may be noted that, although Roman Catholics had refused to co-operate with the Newcastle Commission because no assistant commissioner of their faith was appointed, they were now to be represented by Cardinal Manning and, eventually, the Duke of Norfolk.

By this time, whatever the leaders of the Denominationalists and of their opponents might declaim from platforms at excited public meetings, both sides were compelled to face at least some of the incontrovertible facts. Thus Cardinal Manning observed:

> The most sanguine friends of the voluntary system cannot believe that it will ever recover the whole population of England and Wales; neither can the most devoted advocates of the board school system believe that it can ever extinguish the voluntary system which ... gives freedom to the inextinguishable denominations of our country (*Final Report*, 1888, 244).

When one extremist opponent of school boards put forward a resolution deploring the effect of the Cowper-Temple clause (in its current interpretation) as 'grievously interfering with the proper teaching of revealed truth and ... a serious violation of religious liberty', the motion was heavily defeated, the Bishop of London voting with the majority (ibid., 462).

For their part, those who signed the *Minority Report*, including the veteran R. W. Dale, had regretfully to recognize that,

> this predominance of denominationalism in our national system must continue so long as the majority of the people of our country are willing to delegate the duty of public education to volunteers mainly influenced by denominational zeal.

They considered it understandable that some Nonconformists, incensed at being compelled to send their children to Anglican schools in single-school areas, should want all schools receiving state grants to be controlled by the ratepayers; but they had to point out that,

> having regard to the share in national education now taken by voluntary bodies, it would not be a practical proposal to transfer the whole maintenance and management of all our elementary schools to public representative bodies (ibid., 339, 358).

71

Those who signed the *Minority Report* went even further. The Act of 1870 had required school boards to ensure initially that there was 'efficient and suitable provision' for the elementary education of the children in their districts; thereafter it would be the duty of the boards 'from time to time to provide such additional accommodation as is, in their opinion, necessary'. By 'suitable', Forster had explained, he meant 'schools to which, from the absence of religious or other restriction, parents cannot reasonably object'. But, unsympathetic boards might ask, can parents 'reasonably object' to *any* efficient school, whether established by a school board or even by a different denomination, since the 'conscience clause' applied to them all?

A Minute of the Committee of Council (21 June 1878) had enabled efficient denominational or other schools, if not within a school board district, to qualify for grant simply by existing for at least twelve months under a certificated teacher, with at least thirty children in attendance. The same Minute endeavoured to clear up a disputed interpretation of the Act by ruling that within a school board district any school might be refused a grant by the Education Department if deemed unnecessary, but as to this the Department normally accepted the judgment of the local school board. This curious policy of the state was vividly illustrated by the evidence of P. Cumin, the Secretary of the Department, to the Cross Commission:

> Supposing that there is no deficiency in a place at all, and supposing that a Catholic school is set up in a vigorous nonconformist parish, we first of all say: 'Well, there is no deficiency here; but at the same time if the school board do not object we shall not ... we say ... if you insist upon these children going to a public elementary school and you succeed in emptying that Catholic school, then, of course, there is no deficiency at all, and we agree with the school board....'
> We have asked the school board the question: 'Here are a hundred Catholic children.... Are you going to force them to go to your school?' If they reply: 'Certainly not; we are a great deal too liberal for that,' we say: 'Very well then, the new school will have a grant' (*First Report*, 1886, 655).

There could hardly have been devised a system more likely to lead to controversy and resentment, and there were some examples of flagrant intolerance and injustice, but the outcry and publicity given to these seem to indicate that they were somewhat rare. The *Minority Report* now recommended that annual state grants should be made available for denominational schools wherever there was adequate demand from parents, and that such schools should be freed from the obligation to pay rates. Grants to the existing denominational training colleges were also approved, though Dale and his co-signatories hoped to see in them 'the liberal recognition of the rights of conscience' (*Final Report*, 247, 369, 243).

The alignment for future conflict

Yet between the opposing parties all was far from being 'sweetness and light'. There were not merely all the old underlying causes of resentment already referred to and the by now almost routine complaints of proselytism, evasion of the conscience and Cowper-Temple clauses, and so on. The *Minority Report*, as we have seen, had considered it impossible to put denominational schools under the control of school boards, but it endorsed as 'a more moderate and practicable remedy' the resolution of the General Committee of the Congregational Union in 1888, which, though not demanding the withdrawal of all grants from denominational schools, asked that elementary schools should be provided 'in all parts of the kingdom under the control of the representatives of the public and free from sectarian influence in regard to both management and teaching'. This echo of the Wesleyan call in 1872 for the setting up of school boards in all districts illustrated the resentment of some Nonconformists that in many parts of the country, where the establishment of a school board had been deemed unnecessary, there still were no suitable facilities for Nonconformist children, a hardship all the more resented since such children were not accepted as pupil teachers in Anglican schools and were thus debarred from qualifying for entry to teacher training colleges.

By now the crunch of competition was beginning to be felt. In the years after 1870 the Anglican, Roman Catholic and (to a smaller extent) the Wesleyan authorities made strenuous efforts to establish schools while building grants were still available; and they continued to do so after these ceased. By 1886 about two-thirds of the school places in the state-aided elementary schools were in voluntary schools (and of course there were many in voluntary schools not so aided). But the board schools were beginning to increase more rapidly: of the total increase in registered scholars in state-aided schools since 1870 almost three-fifths had come from board schools, and, since the figures for voluntary schools were now swollen to include those already existing in 1870 but not then in receipt of grant, the actual disproportion was greater than it appeared (calculated from statistics given in C.C., *Final Report*, 1888, 46).

Though many school boards in rural districts were inactive and apathetic, most boards, and especially those in the larger towns, were able and willing to provide more and better schools. The board schools by this time tended to earn higher government grants, though as yet, in spite of superior resources, the disparity here was not very marked: their great advantage arose from being supported by the rates. In 1880 'local exertion' for the voluntary schools produced on average 10s. 9¾d. per child from fees and 7s. 3d. from voluntary contributions; for board schools it produced 9s. od. from fees and 18s. 7d. from rates, so that, in spite of charging higher fees, the voluntary schools received 18s. o¾d., the board schools 27s. 7d.

Furthermore, the difficulties were sometimes even greater than these average figures would imply. The Wesleyan schools relied very much on high fees and little on voluntary contributions; the Roman Catholics could obtain much less than other denominations from fees, and for voluntary contributions they depended greatly on door-to-door collections. In 1880 the average expenditure in Anglican, Wesleyan and British schools (taken together) was roughly 35s. od. for each child in attendance, in board schools it was 42s. od., in Roman Catholic schools 30s. 6d. (calculated from *R.C.C.*, 1880-1, viii). A Conservative government well disposed to denominational schools had in 1876 raised the state grant which *could* be earned for each child to 17s. 6d. (whether other income reached this amount or not), with an additional payment where this could be matched by contributions from other sources; but many of the poorer schools could not earn the maximum grant, whilst others could not raise enough funds to qualify for the grant their results entitled them to, so that money which might have paid an extra teacher was actually deducted from the grant payable.

It is not surprising that Denominationalists complained that rates (including their own) were being spent to provide board schools with better buildings, teachers and equipment, and even, in some cases, with instruction in 'languages, classical and modern, and advanced science'. Incensed by the inducements thus offered to parents to send their children to board schools, supporters of denominational schools claimed that curricula should be 'fixed by the Legislature', not authorized by Codes framed in the Education Department and given legal sanction merely by lying on the tables of the Houses of Parliament unchallenged for one month (*Final Report*, 1888, 145-6). They asked for new state grants towards the cost of improvements and additions to existing facilities where these were required by new regulations; and, using a favourite argument of Cardinal Manning's, they could see no reason why rate aid (to supplement voluntary contributions) should not be given to voluntary schools as it was already given to industrial and reformatory schools, without the imposition of the Cowper-Temple clause. The claim for rate aid, however, was not forcibly expressed, since there was considerable fear, particularly among Anglicans, of demands for local control.

But opponents on the Commission replied in tones which revealed the deep hostility underlying their reluctant acceptance of the existing situation. Payments in aid of repairs and improvements, it was considered, would lead to the renewal of state building grants, and this was unthinkable; whilst the request for rate aid in order to make competition more even was dismissed very bleakly indeed:

> We are of opinion ... that it is unreasonable for voluntary managers to object to the progress of education because their limited means do not allow them to keep up with it. Voluntary management implies voluntary effort, and if the effort is inadequate, there is no duty imposed on them to maintain their schools (*Final Report*, 1888, 372).

6

The Education Act, 1902

The political situation after 1886

By this time an interesting political situation had arisen. The grant of household suffrage in urban areas in 1867, and its extension to rural areas in 1884, led to an increase in the Commons of Radical supporters of the Liberal party. Their leader, Joseph Chamberlain, helped to divide the party by advocating free elementary education and the disestablishment of the Church of England; imperialism, towards which Gladstone was unsympathetic, became another bone of contention; but it was the 'Irish Question' which did most to weaken the Liberals. In 1886 the party split over Gladstone's Bill proposing Home Rule for Ireland; the dissidents, with Chamberlain prominent among them, not only helped to bring down the government but combined to form the Liberal Unionist party. After the ensuing elections seventy-eight of these Unionists held the balance of power in the Commons and threw their weight behind the Conservatives, who held office for all but three (August 1892 – June 1895) of the next nineteen years. In 1891 Chamberlain, so long the most active parliamentary champion of the Nonconformists, became the leader of the Unionists in the Commons. The difficulty of his position was obvious, and in the same year he appealed to his supporters to forget old quarrels, since 'no practical statesman would dare to propose a measure which would be followed by the immediate withdrawal or extinction of the denominational schools' (Garvin, 1933, II, 428). But it was one thing for Nonconformist leaders like Dale and Chamberlain to accept the existing situation, quite another, as the latter well knew, to convince the rank and file.

The Liberals, of course, could look for general support to the grateful Irish Nationalists, but could these be expected to join with Nonconformists to oppose Denominationalism in schools? Many Roman Catholics in England itself, being Irish immigrants or descendants of these, were Irish Nationalists, frequently successfully standing or voting as such even in English local elections

(Burke, 1910, 217-8). The first Roman Catholic member of parliament for Liverpool was an Irish Nationalist who was also returned for Galway (1885). Clearly even within individuals a clash of loyalties was likely. In the elections of 1885 Cardinal Manning had, by implication, urged Roman Catholics to vote for Conservatives (in return for a pledge which later resulted in the appointment of the Cross Commission), but he had felt it necessary to assure the Archbishop of Dublin that there was no intention 'to subordinate the Irish movement to any English question' (quoted McClelland, 1962, 188). Thus each of the groups involved – the two political parties and the different ecclesiastical authorities – was unsure of its allies and uncertain of its strength.

Furthermore, quite apart from ideological preoccupations, all were faced with the intractable circumstances of the existing situation. For, just as Dale and Chamberlain had been obliged to accept the continued existence of denominational schools, the Conservatives were to disappoint many of their supporters by encouraging the spread of board schools. In 1891 the Tories, as the result of an electioneering promise given by Lord Salisbury, the Prime Minister, found themselves committed to 'assisting' education. Salisbury had to be persuaded that it would be impracticable to fulfil the pledge merely by distributing postal orders to children who attended school regularly (Kekewich, 1920, 70); instead, the state accepted the logical consequence of having made elementary education compulsory (in 1880) by passing an Act (1891) which authorized payment of an annual state grant of 10s. 0d. per child (the average fee currently paid by parents) so that fees could either be abolished or be reduced by that amount. A clause in the Act empowered any parent to demand free education for his child and, since voluntary schools could not be compelled to provide this, a further requirement was that where free education would not otherwise be available a new board school (and if necessary a new school board) should be established. Thereupon, according to one disappointed Anglican leader,

> an organised society sent emissaries into neighbourhoods where voluntary schools charged fees, to incite parents to demand free education, and if this could not otherwise be obtained, to insist upon a school board being formed, or an additional board school being erected (Gregory, 1905, 161).

From 1891, following a recommendation made in the *Minority Report* of the Cross Commission, day training colleges connected with universities or university colleges were established by the state, and for many Denominationalists it was a further sad sign of the times that, partly to meet the demands of Nonconformists, no provision was made in them for religious instruction.

Gladstone's persistence with his Home Rule policy continued to weaken the Liberals, and his retirement in 1894 left them in disarray. The general election of 1895 returned to the Commons 340 Conservatives supported by 71 Liberal Unionists in a fully fledged coalition, with Chamberlain as Secretary for the Colonies. The 177 Liberals had as allies 82 Irish Nationalists, so that the government had the comfortable working majority of 152. Naturally, the Denominationalists looked confidently to the Conservatives for assistance, and three demands gradually became particularly insistent: (a) that their schools should receive aid from the rates; (b) that school boards should be abolished in favour of administrative bodies likely to be more sympathetic towards voluntary schools; (c) that there should be provision for denominational instruction in board schools.

Rate aid for denominational schools

Some of those Denominationalists who had signed the *Majority Report* of the Cross Commission had been extremely chary of asking for rate aid for voluntary schools, lest they should be faced with unacceptable demands for control: among those who had expressed fears had been the secretaries of the National Society and of the Catholic Poor School Committee. The recommendation made had therefore been a guarded one:

> That the local education authority should be empowered to supplement from local rates the voluntary subscriptions given to the support of a public state aided elementary school in their district, to an amount equal to these subscriptions but not exceeding ten shillings for each child in average attendance (*Final Report*, 1888, 222).

Cardinal Manning had found the results of accepting rate aid for Roman Catholic industrial schools quite acceptable, and Cardinal Vaughan, his successor, made the demand for rate aid a firm part of official Roman Catholic policy.

But the Anglicans were divided. Though many could see no future for their schools if rate aid continued to be denied, the National Society came out unequivocally against it in 1888, fearing the likelihood of local popular control in areas hostile to the church, and the discouragement of voluntary contributors. The Archbishop of Canterbury, Dr Benson, and Lord Salisbury, were for the same reasons totally opposed to it. However, at the end of a conference arranged by the two archbishops in 1895, the Church of England claimed more freedom to establish denominational schools and greater financial assistance, preferably from taxes, though some readiness was expressed 'to support other definite proposals which would give the necessary relief'. With the death of Archbishop Benson in 1896 such vague language became unnecessary, and in that year a conference attended by the Standing Committee of the National Society, delegates from the Convocations and Houses of Laymen of the Southern and Northern Provinces, and from all the Diocesan Conferences and Boards of Education in the country, made a definite demand for rate aid for voluntary schools within school board districts, to be paid to federations of schools.

On the other hand the qualified and guarded references to rate aid for voluntary schools in the *Majority Report* of the Cross Commission had, predictably, been brusquely rejected in the *Minority Report*, as 'unsound in principle, destructive of the settlement of 1870, and certain, if it became law, to embitter educational politics and intensify sectarian rivalries' (*Final Report*, 1888, 246). (It has for long been a feature of the history of this subject that, however bitterly the passage of an Act of Parliament was contested, those who had opposed it eventually felt entitled, when so disposed, to refer to the Act as a 'settlement' not lightly to be disturbed.)

As usual, fears of those opposed to the denominational system were aroused at any prospect of its receiving support from the rates. In 1888 the National Education Association was founded, with much the same aims as the now defunct National Education League; its purpose was to promote a system of national education 'which shall be efficient, progressive, unsectarian and under popular control' (Armytage, 1951, 275). A. J. Mundella became president, and E. Lyulph Stanley, a member of the London School Board and of the Minority group on the Cross Commission, was appointed chairman of the executive committee. The Association carried on widespread and systematic propaganda. The fears of the Nonconformists helped to make possible an important declaration of unity in 1888. Especially notable, also, was the decision of the Methodists in 1891 to go further than in 1873 by affirming that 'the primary objective of Methodist policy' was 'the establishment of school boards everywhere ... and the placing of a Christian unsectarian school within a reasonable distance of every family, especially in rural districts' (quoted Cruickshank, 1963, 60). Coming from the dissenting sect closest to the Anglicans, and one which still maintained denominational schools, this was significant, though it did not mean the abandonment of Wesleyan schools. But gradually they came to charge relatively high fees, to rely little on public subscriptions, and to cater for children whose parents (many not Wesleyans) were prepared to pay for somewhat 'superior' schooling. Even so, after 1890 the numbers on the rolls of Wesleyan schools began to decline.

The need to oppose rate aid for denominational schools, combined with continued anger over the difficulties encountered in some single-school areas and repugnance for the 'Romish' practices of a growing number of Anglican clergymen, helped the Nonconformists, including even the Wesleyans, to draw closer together. From 1892 a congress of the 'Free Churches' was held annually, and in 1896 the National Council of the Evangelical Free Churches took definite shape. The Free Churches now claimed to have a combined membership greater than that of the Established Church and to have more accommodation for worshippers and more children attending their Sunday schools (Halévy, III, 1950, 175). Henceforward it became common to speak of the Free Churches and of the 'Nonconformist conscience' as if what was held in common had come to matter far more than what had divided the Protestant dissenters.

Denominational instruction in board schools

We have noted that, although the state had decreed in 1870 that religious instruction need not be given in board schools, and that, if given, it might (with certain minimal safeguards) be denominational, almost all board schools in fact provided some form of religious instruction which was considered to be undenominational. As the numbers of children attending board schools increased and threatened eventually to surpass those in denominational schools, the Anglican authorities, in particular, saw the need to gain some foothold in the board schools if their influence in the field of elementary education was to be maintained. The school boards and the Nonconformists naturally fought to continue what was now taken to be their traditional policy, as sanctioned by law, but just as important was the widespread resistance of teachers to any infringement of their freedom which might arise from religious tests, and any lowering of their status implied in permitting others to give religious instruction in the schools.

A particularly significant dispute occurred in London in 1894 after an Anglican member of the school board complained that a teacher in a board school had accepted without comment a child's statement that the father of Jesus was Joseph. Since Denominationalists happened to be in a majority on the board, it was decided, after heated debates, to inform teachers that the board could not approve of any teaching which denied either the divine or the human nature of Christ, or which left 'on the minds of the children any other impression than that they were bound to trust and

serve Him as their God and Lord'. Teachers who could not accept
this ruling would not be penalized but would be relieved of the
task of giving religious instruction. Thereupon more than 3,000
teachers asked to be so relieved, most of them as a matter of
principle, and they ultimately carried their point. The bitter controversy aroused, and its outcome, were not soon forgotten: suc-
ceeding governments were extremely wary of proceeding without
taking into account the views of the representatives of the teachers,
and the National Union of Teachers was careful to have spokesmen
in the Commons. The Archbishops' Conference of 1895, already
referred to, could therefore hardly have been hopeful when it asked
that 'all reasonable facilities shall be afforded for the separate
religious instruction of children of Board or Voluntary schools,
whose parents may desire it, in the spirit of the Industrial Schools
Act of 1866'.

The new local authorities

In 1870, as we have seen, it had been found necessary to entrust
the local administration of rate-supported schools to boards specially
elected for the purpose, because provision for local government
outside the large boroughs was so rudimentary, and was objected
to as being largely in the hands of the landed gentry and those
under their influence. But in many areas school boards did not
exist, even by 1890, or they were inefficient, mainly because of
lack of local interest in the education of the poor. Administrators
complained of a system which permitted boards to spend rates
which they were not directly responsible for levying. Matthew
Arnold was not alone in believing that 'the real preliminary to
an effective system of popular education is, in fact, to provide the
country with an effective municipal organisation' (1868, 274).

In 1888 the Local Government Act had provided a much more
efficient administrative system than any existing hitherto, largely
because of the need to cope with the expanding social services:
there were to be sixty-one 'county councils', elected by household
suffrage, whilst the corporations of boroughs with more than 50,000
inhabitants were to act as 'county borough councils' in their own
right. Many Denominationalists were anxious to see the end of
school boards, regarding them as being, in most large towns, hostile
to voluntary schools and financially irresponsible, whilst Conservative supporters in general objected to them as strongholds
of Radicalism. On the other hand, those who supported the boards
praised their efficiency in the larger towns and cities such as
London, and feared the consequences of handing over control of
board schools to large county councils likely to be dominated by

Conservative Anglicans.

Governments moved with extreme caution. In 1889 the new councils were empowered to provide from the rates grants for technical and manual instruction in schools other than elementary schools: from 1890 government funds were made available for grants to such schools in aid of technical education, this eventually being defined in such a way as to include almost all of the subjects normally taught in secondary schools. Within a few years many of the new authorities were availing themselves of these powers. This division of control in the field of education was naturally disliked by most educational administrators, and there was clearly a danger that for political and administrative reasons (to say nothing of the pressure from those who detested school boards on religious grounds) the boards would soon be taken over.

Generally speaking, therefore, one might say that by 1896 the battle lines were drawn up, with the war aims clear to both sides, the Conservatives unassailable in parliament, the Liberals anxious for the conflict, if only to rally their divided forces, the Denominationalists and their opponents each united for action, and the teachers forewarned and conscious of their strength; but both political parties had doubts about their allies, and the administrators had yet to speak.

Preliminary skirmishes in parliament

In 1896 the government introduced a Bill which would have abolished the limit on the amount of state grant which could be obtained by denominational schools without corresponding voluntary contributions, increased the grants to such schools and to necessitous board schools, exempted voluntary schools from the payment of rates, and limited the amounts which school boards could raise from the rates. More important, as departures from established policy, were the proposals: (*a*) to permit 'reasonable arrangements' for separate denominational instruction in both voluntary and board schools where a sufficient number of parents of a given denomination so desired; and (*b*) to empower county and borough councils to supervise the work of secondary and technical schools, and even, *where school boards agreed*, to take over board schools.

The widespread opposition aroused by the Bill, differences of opinion among Anglicans about some of its provisions, inept handling by the government, and strong criticism by teachers who feared the introduction of religious tests, all combined to cause the withdrawal of the Bill. In the following year (1897), a much less ambitious measure was passed to exempt voluntary schools from the payment of rates and increase state grants to them. Supporters of school boards were alerted, however, when county and county borough councils were recognized as the local education authorities for secondary education, except where this was carried on in elementary schools.

New attitudes towards education and welfare

But the time for this kind of tinkering had long passed. Leaving all other considerations aside, the pressure of commercial and industrial competition from abroad was greater than ever, yet Britain, still without a national system of secondary education, was saddled with a divided elementary system each part of which had great numbers of supporters convinced of the need to limit the effectiveness of the other, and more than half of which could not be adequately financed, simply because of differences in religious and political beliefs. Most of the old ideas on which the existing arrangements had been based had been, or were being, tacitly or explicitly rejected by all but the most reactionary clerics or politicians: *laissez faire*, reliance on parental responsibility, the fear of state domination through the schools, the need to encourage voluntary contributions, insistence on monopoly control by the clergy, the subordinate rôle to be assigned to teachers, and, most outdated of all, the adequacy of elementary instruction for the children of the poor. Moreover in many industries there was now less demand for child labour and much greater need for entrants capable of being trained for skilled work in manufacture or commerce.

A strong sense of the potential of the state to express the best inclinations of its members in ways not available to individuals was finding expression in diverse forms, among them the political activity of working-class and intellectual Socialists, Christian Socialism, Fabianism, the teachings of T. H. Green and Bernard Bosanquet – and of course the body of social legislation already in existence. 'Socialism' in the sense of state intervention was no longer a term to arouse widespread apprehension: the 'State Socialism' of Bismarck had helped to make the word, and the idea, comparatively respectable. In 1885 Joseph Chamberlain had declared:

> The Poor Law is Socialism; the Education Act is Socialism; the greater part of municipal work is Socialism; and every kindly act of legislation by which the community has sought to discharge its responsibilities and obligations to the poor is Socialism; but it is none the worse for that (quoted Maccoby, 1938, 303).

83

Administrators made necessary and powerful by the complexity of modern government and the inadequacy of amateur politicians found that they had much in common with modern Socialists of the stamp of Sidney Webb (himself, significantly, an able and experienced administrator) or Bernard Shaw – men apt to think of Socialism as primarily the prevention of what the former called 'muddle' and the latter 'waste'.

The administrative 'muddle'

As a result of the conflicts of politicians and religious groups (and of the compromises made to avoid them) administrators at the end of the century were in fact faced with something akin to chaos. The Education Department had to correspond separately with more than 2,500 school boards and with the managers of more than 20,000 voluntary schools. Among its manifold duties were the annual assessment of grants and the inspection of schools on which these were based. Moreover, grants to schools of various kinds were made also by the Charity Commissioners, the Science and Art Department and even, where appropriate subjects were taught, the Board of Agriculture. Some progress towards unifying the central authority was made in 1899, when an Act was passed to establish in 1900 a Board of Education with power to take over the educational functions of these various bodies. The President of the Board was entrusted with 'the superintendence of matters relating to education in England and Wales'. Since from the beginning, according to the Duke of Devonshire, the first President, it was 'perfectly well understood that there would be no board at all', pardonable curiosity prompted a parliamentary question as to why it had in theory been created; the Duke, though convinced there had been a reason, was quite unable to remember it (*Hansard*, LXX, 353).

On the local level, even apart from the important political considerations and the difficulty of dealing with so many boards or separate schools, administrators were faced with two main problems. The first was the policy to be adopted towards the voluntary schools: were they to be allowed to founder for lack of adequate financial support or, if not, how were they to be assisted? It was to be expected that, like their predecessors Kay-Shuttleworth and Forster in a similar situation, administrators would reject the first possibility, if only because of the enormous cost of replacing voluntary schools, and that they would favour some means of support for these which would make unnecessary recurring appeals for greater assistance, and lead to more unified control of elementary education.

A second problem was connected with the administration of secondary education, in so far as this was financed from public funds. In 1897, as we have seen, the new councils had been given powers over the secondary education not provided in elementary schools; but a great deal of such education was in fact given in elementary schools controlled by school boards and supported from the rates; for the great range of ability among children in such schools had led to the development of 'higher grade' schools and special classes catering for relatively advanced work. Since the Act of 1870 had vaguely defined an elementary school as one in which 'elementary education is the principal part of the education there given', the legality of this policy was open to question. But in any case, once again, the administrator's professional inclination to make one blade of grass grow where two grew before would predispose him to favour unified control. Should all aided secondary education be controlled by the new councils or by school boards? Whichever authority was chosen should it also be responsible for all aided elementary education, and, if so, what degree of control should be exercised over voluntary schools in return for assured financial support from the rates?

Matters were brought to a head quite deliberately, very largely at the prompting of Sir John Gorst, Vice-President of the Committee of Council, and his private secretary, Robert Morant. Interested parties were encouraged to challenge the right of the London School Board to spend rates on secondary education and the instruction of adults in evening classes; following an adverse report from a local government auditor, Cockerton, the courts finally ruled in 1901 that it was illegal for a school board to spend rates on the education of students older than about sixteen and on much of the advanced instruction which had in the past been given in elementary schools. The government's hand was forced: it must clearly make new and more systematic provision for education other than elementary, and decide whether councils or school boards or both should be authorized to provide it.

The proposed 'way out'

Morant had studied carefully the educational administration in France and Switzerland and was determined to bring order out of chaos in Britain. His energy, diplomacy and great administrative ability gave him influence among politicians greater than his rank at first warranted, though he was quickly promoted to a post in the Secondary Schools Branch of the Board of Education (August 1900), and became Acting Secretary of the Board in November 1902 and Secretary in April 1903. In formulating his policies he was

85

undoubtedly much influenced by the Fabian Socialist, Sidney Webb, who had an intimate knowledge of the working of the London School Board and was the chairman of the recently established Technical Instruction Committee of the London County Council. The Fabian pamphlet CVI *The Education Muddle and the Way Out*, was at least largely Webb's work, and its advocacy of local control of all forms of education by a single large authority was extremely cogent: the new county councils should normally become the local education authorities for their areas, and should have powers to assist and control the voluntary schools, which were 'often starving for lack of funds, and grossly below any reasonable standard of educational efficiency'. The continued existence of the voluntary schools was accepted, and, somewhat surprisingly, even welcomed:

> It is politically impossible to abolish these voluntary schools; and whatever we may think of the theological reasons for their establishment, their separate and practically individual management does incidentally afford what ought to be, in any public system of education, most jealously guarded, namely, variety and the opportunity of experiment (p. 14).

It would be necessary

> to put such schools under the control of the local education authority; to improve and strengthen their committees of management; to raise their efficiency and especially to provide better salaries for their teachers; to make impossible the tyrannical vagaries of foolish clergymen in the village schools; and to bring these into co-ordination with the rest of the educational system (ibid.).

When it came to definite proposals, however, the pamphlet undermined its own case, to a degree that seems not generally to have been recognized, by declaring that there were 'about 47 County Boroughs in which, as in London, the School Board System may be deemed to have so firmly established itself as to be entitled to be untouched', and in these large towns, therefore, the town councils should become the authorities only for that education which lay 'outside the power of the School Boards' (p.15).

In spite of this inconsistency Morant appreciated how admirably the establishment of new all-purpose authorities could solve the immediate problems of: (*a*) providing for secondary and technical education – and even teacher training; (*b*) ensuring that efficient elementary education was available where school boards did not exist, or were ineffective; and (*c*) obtaining financial security for the voluntary schools, and thereby not only following his personal inclinations but also winning powerful support for the whole comprehensive policy. In a memorandum prepared for the cabinet he wrote:

> The only way to 'get up steam' for passing any Education Bill at all in the teeth of School Board opposition will be to include in it some scheme for aiding denominational schools (Allen, 1934, 153).

He determined that all school boards must go, even the powerful and efficient London School Board being reprieved only temporarily. He established close contact with the Anglican and Roman Catholic authorities, and it was typical of his thoroughness that he should carefully choose, and persuade, to champion his policy in parliament the most skilful and resolute parliamentarian of his day, A. J. Balfour, whose own sympathies were not in doubt, since as late as 1885 he was echoing the language used by Forster in 1870:

> I entirely deny that the Board school is the normal and proper system of managing education. I consider that it is, and ought to be, merely the supplement to voluntary schools when voluntary schools fail to do their duty (Gregory, 1905, 167).

The Anglican proposals

The pressure from the Church of England was very powerful, especially since the leader of the High Church party, and its spokesman in the Commons, was the Prime Minister's son, Lord Hugh Cecil. In 1901 the National Society demanded that in denominational schools the cost of all teaching except religious instruction should be paid by the state and that the various religious bodies should be allowed to give denominational instruction in board schools. A joint conference of the Convocations of Canterbury and York in July 1901 made proposals significantly close to those later adopted by the government: (a) that though the religious bodies might be expected to provide their own schools and pay for necessary alterations, structural repairs and extensions, other costs of maintenance should come from taxes or rates; (b) the schools should be governed and teachers appointed and dismissed by existing boards of managers, supplemented by up to one-third of the total number of representatives of the local authority; (c) denominational instruction should be made available in all elementary schools (if parents so requested).

In December of the same year the Bishop of Rochester informed the Prime Minister that the 'intolerable strain' which Balfour had earlier referred to was now 'at *breaking point*' – that if the church's schools were 'not in some way relieved in this next session' many would go within the year – enough greatly to weaken the cause, and, by creating the impression that the 'game is up', to bring down others 'in increasing numbers and an accelerating rate (*sic*)' (Allen, 1934, 163).

The contribution of aided voluntary schools and training colleges

It may be of interest to examine briefly the position of the voluntary schools and training colleges as the government was being urged to change the basis of their financial support. The figures which follow relate only to inspected public day elementary schools, excluding special schools, in England and Wales for the year ending 31 August 1902. Overall, there were now places for 20·25 per cent of the estimated total population, as compared with 8·75 in 1870. During this period the amount of voluntary subscriptions for erecting, enlarging or improving schools had been 'at least £12,000,000'.

It is noteworthy that although since 1870 nearly 1400 voluntary schools had been transferred to school boards (including 981 Anglican, 26 Wesleyan and 272 British schools), the proportion of voluntary to board schools was still as high as 71 to 29; but since many of the voluntary schools were very small the percentage of children on the rolls was about 52·5 in voluntary schools as against 47·5 in board schools. Moreover, as indicating the more favourable siting and amenities of the modern board schools, of the accommodation in them 94 per cent was in use as opposed to only 82·5 per cent in the voluntary schools (as shown by the number of children on the rolls). The amount subscribed for voluntary schools was in 1901-2 higher than ever before, and the amount per child in attendance higher than in every year except one for the last twenty years, but it now represented a little more than a quarter of the annual expenditure, with very little coming from fees. The most revealing figures were those for the annual 'cost of maintenance' of a child: in a board school, just over £3; in a voluntary school, a little over £2 6s. od. (Figures are taken or calculated from *R.B.E.* 1902-3.)

Of the students in the residential teacher training colleges in 1901-2, 68·6 per cent were in Anglican and 6·4 per cent in Roman Catholic colleges, whilst 25 per cent were in colleges (Wesleyan, British and undenominational) which would admit Nonconformists. Lloyd George complained in 1902 that 'only one-twentieth of the expense of maintaining Anglican colleges was provided by the subscriptions of the Anglican Church', the rest coming from government grants and students' fees (*Hansard*, CVII, 1104). The new day training colleges had extended the opportunities for Nonconformists to become teachers: if the places in them are included, 49·5 per cent of students were in Anglican and 4·7 per cent in Roman Catholic colleges, whilst 45·8 per cent would admit Nonconformists. It must be remembered, however, that British and undenominational colleges imposed no religious test for entry and admitted considerable numbers of Anglicans (in one such college referred to in parliament the proportion was as high as one-third – *Hansard*, CVII, 1176); this, of course, reduced the number of places actually available to Nonconformists. Again, as we have noted, Nonconformists felt aggrieved that in many single-school areas their children could not take the initial step towards entering the profession, since Anglican schools would not accept them as pupil teachers.

Joseph Chamberlain and the Nonconformists

In 1900 a general election, held when the Boer War appeared near to a victorious conclusion, continued the Conservatives in power with a comfortable overall majority of 134. The Liberals were now more divided than ever because of the war, and their allies, the Irish Nationalists, were prepared to vote with the Conservatives in support of denominational schools. As Colonial Secretary, Joseph Chamberlain had won great personal prestige during the war, and the support of his followers was important to the government, but Chamberlain well knew that he owed much of that support to the Nonconformists, that if he alienated them he would be lost, and that it was now far too late to break with the Conservatives and rejoin the Liberals. With their customary large majority in the Lords, the Conservatives were well placed for decisive action.

Yet the government was by no means resolute. Many, like Lord Salisbury, were fearful of losing Unionist support, and he, the Chancellor of the Exchequer and some other members of the Cabinet were moved also by reluctance to increase the rates in order to assist denominational schools, either on principle or on grounds of economy. Moreover it was obvious that parliamentary majorities might mean little in a long and bitter contest over conscientious refusals to pay rates. The Cabinet changed its mind and its plans repeatedly (Fitzroy, I, 63, 67-8). But the pressure of the Denominationalists, and particularly, of course, of the Anglicans, was unyielding; the need for action could not be denied, and Morant was on hand to counter all evasions. When Gorst and Chamberlain revived the proposal to allow individual ratepayers to decide how their payments for education should be allocated it was pointed out that many poor people paid no rates, whilst large undertakings could have no religious views. The proposal, accepted even by many Anglicans, that the churches themselves should pay for Denominational teaching, was judged unworkable. When Chamberlain, in desperation, asked why additional grants could not come from the state, Morant, bluntly and unanswerably, replied, 'Because your War has made further recourse to State grants impossible' (Allen, 1934, 168). It appears, however, that Chamberlain did obtain an undertaking that the wide-spread hostility to the abolition of school boards and to rate aid for denominational schools would be recognized by a provision that no local authority would take over a school board or give rate aid without the sanction of the ratepayers.

This did not save Chamberlain from the resentment of many of his Nonconformist friends. Chamberlain could only reply that he had hoped in 1870 to adopt 'the only fair and logical system, the entire separation between religious and secular education'. But the system had been tried in Birmingham, had failed, 'and was ultimately abandoned owing to the overwhelming pressure of the Nonconformists themselves, who refused to accept an entirely secular system'. Now, 'as practical educationalists', they must consider what was possible: the denominational schools existed and could not be replaced. They must rely on some representation of ratepayers on committees of management and the local option to refuse support from rates (*The Times*, 24 April 1902).

The Bill in parliament

The government's Bill, introduced by Balfour in March 1902, was before the Commons for longer than any previous Bill in history (fifty-seven days); in spite of the government's overwhelming majority, the 'guillotine' procedure had to be invoked to complete its passage. The Nonconformists and many others saw the proposals to abolish the school boards and give rate aid to denominational schools as ensuring the permanent subsidization of the Established and Roman Catholic Churches; and passions were particularly inflamed when Lord Hugh Cecil made the long-remembered remark:

> a board school is a school with only one door; the child goes in, learns a great deal that is valuable, and goes out again into the street. A church school, a Wesleyan school, or a Roman Catholic school are schools with two doors, and the other door leads on into the Church or Chapel (*Hansard*, CVII, 845).

He was answered by a Nonconformist member: 'The noble Lord ... says the object of the elementary school is to turn out Churchmen; we think it is to turn out citizens' (ibid., 851).

The hostility of the Nonconformists inside and outside the House was unbounded and well organized. It was expressed particularly forcefully up and down the country by Dr Clifford (Baptist), and by the Rev. Hugh Price Hughes (Wesleyan), who spoke of Nonconformists refusing to pay the education rate. The Liberal party naturally welcomed the opportunity to unite their ranks and resume the old contest; David Lloyd George was particularly eloquent in denunciation and he appealed (in vain) to Irish Nationalists to help Welsh Nonconformists to fight English clerical domination, as the Liberals had tried to help the Irish to obtain Home Rule (*Hansard*, CVII, 1111). The attacks dealt with the now traditional topics, objections to paying rates for the support of a 'false religion', proselytism in denominational schools, the more than 8,000 single-school areas, the appointment and promotion of teachers on religious grounds in schools financed from rates, inadequate public control of denominational schools and so on; but particular prominence was given to the claim of Nonconformists for equal opportunities to become teachers.

In parliament few voices were now raised in favour either of making provision for religious instruction compulsory, or of purely secular education. Outside, many in the growing Socialist and Labour movements were chary of taking part in a contest between rival creeds and saw the bitter controversy as demonstrating 'the need for a purely secular system of education' (Simon, 1965, 231). There was great anxiety to prevent the abolition of the school boards and their higher grade schools, which had extended the opportunities open to able working-class children, and there was much opposition to clerical control of schools; the Trades Union Congress, in a circular issued in 1900, stressed these points and asked that education should be 'unsectarian' (ibid., 199). The great disappointment to the Liberals was their 'betrayal' by the National Union of Teachers, which supported the Bill because it 'envisaged a comprehensive, unified scheme of education under a single central authority with a single local authority in each district', and also because of the financial help promised towards the salaries of teachers in voluntary schools (Tropp, 1957, 181).

Two features of the progress of the Bill deserve particular attention. Balfour, who became Prime Minister in July 1902, was under intense pressure from the Denominationalists and their supporters within his party to *compel* local authorities to take over school boards and assist voluntary schools from the rates. He yielded so far as to permit a free vote of the House: the majority in favour of compulsion was overwhelming, and Chamberlain's humiliation was complete. The second event was all the more interesting because of this result: the passing of an amendment moved by a Colonel Kenyon – Slaney removing control of the religious education in denominational schools from the local clergy and vesting it in the managers, clerical and lay together. This was intended to curb the powers of clergymen inclined to 'ritualist' and 'Romish' practices but it aroused quite unmeasured protests from the clergy. Nevertheless it passed on a free vote by a large majority, and this lack of sympathy for clerical feelings in a House so well disposed towards denominational schools led one contemporary diarist to observe:

> It is curious that a Bill in the conduct of which the Government have exposed themselves to bitter attacks for their alleged surrender to ecclesiastical pressure should have been the occasion of a most remarkable demonstration of the little hold clerical influence has on the temper of the House of Commons (Fitzroy, 1926, 1, 113).

The Lords were more sympathetic and ensured that, when managers disagreed, the bishop, where he already had the final decision on doctrine (as in schools in union with the National Society), would retain it. The Roman Catholic clergy, for their part, had little reason to fear that their own followers on management boards would dispute their rulings in the field of religious instruction.

Chief provisions of the Act

It may be helpful to summarize here the most important relevant provisions of the Education Act of 1902, which was extended to London in 1903. (Though schools provided and maintained wholly from public funds became legally known as 'provided' schools from 1902 and 'county' schools from 1944, they will henceforward be referred to in this book by the more self-explanatory and commonly used name of 'council' schools.)

> (1) The councils of the counties and county boroughs became local education authorities (as also did some of the larger borough and urban district councils, though with restricted powers).
> (2) The local education authorities took over in the field of elementary education the powers hitherto exercised by the school boards and school attendance committees, but they were also given control over the secular education in voluntary schools.
> (3) The authorities were empowered to 'take such steps as seemed to them desirable' (within certain financial limits and after consultation with the Board of Education) 'to supply, or aid the supply of education other than elementary and to promote the general co-ordination of all forms of education'. They were hence enabled, among other things, to spend rate income on secondary schools and training colleges, thus increasing the number of such

establishments which were undenominational and available for Nonconformists.

(4) It would be the duty of each local authority to 'maintain and keep efficient' all the public elementary schools in its area; in both voluntary and council schools the cost of running the school and of providing instruction, secular and religious, would be met from government grants and local rates. The managing bodies of voluntary schools would normally comprise not more than four members representing those providing the school and not more than two representing the local authority: these managers would have to 'carry out any directions of the authority as to the secular instruction to be given' and the number and qualifications of the teachers to be employed. Teachers would be appointed and dismissed by the managers, though the authority's approval would be required except where dismissal was 'on grounds connected with the giving of religious instruction'. As small concessions to Nonconformists, managers were empowered to depart from the provisions of a school's trust deed by appointing teachers without reference to denominational beliefs (except in the case of a head teacher), and where there were more applicants than vacancies for posts as pupil teachers the appointments would be made by the authority.

(5) In return for the right to give denominational instruction and to ensure the appointment of suitable teachers, the voluntary body would be obliged to provide the school building, keep the structure in good repair, and make such 'alterations and improvements' in the buildings as might be 'reasonably required' by the authority; but the latter would make good any damage which it considered to be due to 'fair wear and tear'.

(6) The ultimate decision whether a new council or voluntary school would best meet the needs of an area would rest with the Board of Education, which would 'have regard to the interest of secular instruction, the wishes of parents ... and to the economy of the rates'; but, generally speaking, a school once recognized could not be declared 'unnecessary' and be deprived of aid from public funds, unless the average attendance fell below thirty.

The chief provisions relating to religious instruction were as follows:

(1) In a denominational school or college which received aid from the local authority no pupil might be compelled to receive religious instruction either in the school or elsewhere; the permitted times for religious instruction were no longer prescribed as being at the end and/or beginning of the school meeting but must be 'conveniently arranged for the purpose of allowing the withdrawal' of pupils where desired. This vaguer formula favoured those who wished to foster a distinctively denominational 'atmosphere' throughout the school day.

(2) In a 'school, college or hostel' provided by a local education

authority no 'catechism or formulary distinctive of any particular religious denomination' should be taught; but the authority, at the request of parents, and under such conditions and at such times as it thought desirable, might permit 'any religious instruction' to be given, provided that 'no unfair preference' was given to any denomination and no expense was thereby incurred by the authority. (The practical difficulties entailed in complying with these provisos will be appreciated.)

(3) As indicated earlier, the Kenyon-Slaney amendment provided that religious instruction in denominational schools must be in accordance with the original trust deeds and controlled by the managers as a whole (though the ruling whether the instruction was in fact so in accordance might continue to be given by the bishop or other superior ecclesiastical authority, where the trust deeds so prescribed).

The conscientious objectors

Without extensive quotation it is impossible to convey to a modern reader an adequate impression of the extraordinary antagonism and bitterness aroused by the discussion and passage of the 1902 Act; it may be illustrated on the one hand by the great demonstration on Woodhouse Moor outside Leeds, where 'from five separate platforms the patriarchs of Nonconformity admonished and exhorted a vast concourse, assembled by special excursion trains from all over the country' (Amery, 1951, IV, 495), and, on the other hand, by the Anglican clergyman who declared the Kenyon-Slaney amendment 'to be the greatest betrayal since the Crucifixion', adding that 'he would rather the Colonel should have seduced his wife rather than come to Parliament with such a proposal' (Fitzroy, 1926, I, 112).

The threat that many Nonconformists would refuse to pay rates for denominational schools was duly carried out, especially in Wales, but it proved difficult for individuals to resist for long an Act of Parliament. More serious was the defiance of some local authorities. In England, for example, the West Riding County Council had to be legally restrained from reducing teachers' salaries by the amount estimated to be earned while giving religious instruction (Beales, 1950, 386). In Wales, with its vast Nonconformist majority, opposition was particularly intense, and Professor Eaglesham (1962) has classified the types of resistance attempted by various councils, including the 'repudiation policy', by which the council simply ignored the existence of denominational schools, and the 'slow starvation plan', which took advantage of the fact that the Act did not specify at what standard the voluntary schools should be 'maintained', so that they could be left to manage on government grants without support from rates. The government retaliated with the Authorities Default Act (1904) empowering it to repay expenses incurred by school managers and deduct the amount from the grant payable to the local authority. Even so, sporadic hostilities continued until the need for them seemed to have ended with the general election of 1906.

7

Attempts to modify the 'settlement' of 1902

The Liberal Bills of 1906-8

The Liberals gained an overwhelming victory in the general election of 1906, largely over the issue of Free Trade v Protection but partly because of continuing hostility to the Act of 1902, as the Conservatives were quick to recognize and very slow to forget. The long rule of the Tories had ended, and once again, as in 1868, many Free Churchmen and other Liberal supporters looked confidently to the new government for sweeping changes in educational legislation. Once again they were disappointed, to some extent because the House of Lords remained very largely Conservative and strong in support of the Established Church, but – more fundamentally important – chiefly because of the continued impossibility of drastically altering the existing system without either incurring great expenditure on additional schools or applying coercion on a vast scale.

Of course the Liberals were well aware of the difficulties of defying conscientious objections, but underlying their proposals was the conviction that, generally speaking, the demand for Protestant denominational instruction in schools arose almost entirely from the Anglican clergy, not from working-class parents: during the parliamentary debates in 1902 the president of the National Union of Teachers had been several times quoted as declaring, somewhat sweepingly, that 'Protestant parents of this country do not care a farthing for dogmatic religion' (*Hansard*, CVII, 1009). Similar opinions were frequently expressed and rarely vigorously contested. But it was felt to be otherwise with Roman Catholic (and Jewish) parents. If, therefore, special arrangements acceptable to these could be made, a just solution to the religious difficulty would be relatively easy to find. This was no new proposal: it had been made by Richard Cobden as long ago as 1839 (Murphy, 1959, 204), by those who signed the *Minority Report* of the Cross Commission in 1888 (*Final Report*, 363), and by many others. The trouble, of course, was that favourable treatment of the Roman Catholics would be resented by many Anglicans and Free Churchmen, whilst some Roman Catholic leaders saw dangers in becoming isolated from the politically powerful Established Church.

Between 1906 and 1908 the Liberals introduced three important Education Bills, designed, as far as possible, to fulfil their election pledges (a fourth, McKenna's unsuccessful Bill of 1907, merely proposed to compel denominational managers to pay one-fifteenth of their teachers' salaries, this representing the supposed cost of giving denominational instruction). In each of the three Bills there was provision for the compulsory transference to the local education authorities of voluntary schools in single-school areas; and each Bill set out to ensure: (*a*) public control of most of the other voluntary schools, by transference or otherwise; (*b*) restriction of the amount of denominational instruction given at public expense; and (*c*) strict limitation of the number of teachers whose appointment, promotion or retention of their posts could legally be affected by their religious beliefs.

Augustine Birrell's Bill of 1906 was based on the assumption that if denominational instruction were to be given only where it was specifically requested by parents its provision need be much less widespread and would arouse much less animosity among those many Free Churchmen who saw such instruction as mainly designed to win adherents to the Established Church. The Bill proposed that all voluntary schools should be transferred and rented to local education authorities *if these agreed to accept them*: this local option would allow consideration to be given to the conscientious scruples of ratepayers. Normally, as in the existing council schools, undenominational instruction would be given; however, if the authority consented, denominational instruction could be provided twice a week where parents wished their children to receive it, though the regular teachers must not give it. There might be also, in some schools taken over, more extended provision for denominational instruction, to be given daily by the regular teachers, but this only where: (*a*) the authority gave consent; (*b*) the school was in an urban area with more than 5,000 inhabitants; (*c*) at least four-fifths of the parents so desired.

It is hardly surprising that these proposals found few supporters, since many Nonconformists opposed any continuation of support for Denominationalism and most Denominationalists naturally resented the restrictions imposed, in particular dependence on the decisions of local education authorities, who might simply refuse to take over responsibility for schools. Amendments limiting the power of authorities to refuse denominational instruction alienated the one side without satisfying the other; but the Bill passed the Commons with a large majority. In the Lords, however, political opposition and the influence of the Established Church were so great that the Bill was altered out of all recognition in favour of the Denominationalists, and a threatened constitutional battle between Lords and Commons inflamed the passions of extremists outside parliament. The Liberals made concessions, reducing the proportion of parents whose consent would be required for a school to have 'extended' denominational facilities, and ensuring the employment of suitable teachers to give instruction in such a school; whilst in the schools having more restricted denominational facilities ordinary teachers might be allowed to *volunteer* to give such instruction, except in single-school areas. The Roman Catholics were prepared to accept the modified proposals, and the Church of England authorities came close to doing so; but the Conservative party was adamant in its resistance. The Lords rejected the amended Bill and no solution was possible.

McKenna's Bill of 1908 had at least the merit of simplicity: (*a*) all schools in single-school areas would be taken over by the local education authorities, denominational instruction being permitted in them if given by volunteers after school hours; (*b*) the managers of other voluntary schools could choose whether to surrender their schools and lose the right to give denominational instruction, or to retain them, thus preserving that right but forfeiting rate aid and those services ancillary to education provided by the local authority – they would thus revert to the position prior to 1902, receiving a government grant and being allowed to charge fees. These proposals came to nothing.

Runciman's Bill of the same year, as amended, again allowed for the transference of voluntary schools to local authorities or for 'contracting out'. It was hoped that the majority of the schools 'contracting out' and retaining full freedom of action with regard to religious instruction would be Roman Catholic; they would receive state grants but could have no guarantee of future financial security. Most voluntary schools, it was hoped, would become council schools and, as a *quid pro quo*, the state would permit denominational instruction to be given twice a week in *all* council schools, by instructors from outside the schools or by those regular teachers who volunteered to give it – though, to meet the objections of some Free Churchmen and teachers' organizations, no head teacher subsequently appointed might do so. Denominational instruction would not be paid for from public funds. Many Anglicans were won over by the prospect of having assured facilities for Anglican teaching in so many of the nation's schools at a time when the numbers in their own schools were falling, but others were alarmed at the prospect of losing control of their schools; the Roman Catholics feared the long-term consequences of separation from the national system; whilst many teachers in council schools suspected that they would in practice be pressed to give denominational instruction, and they were opposed to permitting to others 'the right of entry' to give such instruction. Moreover, the National Union of Teachers had supported the Bill of 1902 largely because it ensured better pay and working conditions for teachers in impoverished voluntary schools; there naturally was now opposition to any arrangement compelling or permitting voluntary schools to 'contract out', at the risk of receiving reduced financial support.

In the face of such opposition, and that of their sincerely convinced or merely opportunist political opponents, the Liberals had to recognize that even a large majority in the Commons could not ensure victory in this difficult and dangerous field. Their most important success was achieved by an administrative change of regulations intended to make training for teaching more accessible to Nonconformists. The establishment of the undenominational day training and local authority colleges had helped in this respect, and regulations introduced in 1907, and amended in 1908, now provided that in the selection of candidates for one-half of the number of places in a denominational college the governors must not reject a candidate because of his religious faith or refusal to undertake to attend religious worship, observance or instruction; in colleges recognized for grant since 1907 religious instruction might be given only to those students who wished to receive it, whilst no member of the staff might be required to belong, or not to belong, to any particular denomination. The regulations were not difficult to evade, since discrimination was feared and was difficult to establish, meetings for worship often concluded with routine announcements of importance to students, most students not Roman Catholics had no wish to attend Roman Catholic colleges, and so on; still, the state could claim that it had done all in its power to remove one of the chief grievances of Nonconformists.

But on the whole the efforts of the Liberals had served only to anger the most extreme of their disappointed followers and to arouse animosity and suspicion among Denominationalists, who had shown themselves just as capable of threatening to withhold rates as their opponents had earlier been. Many people were tired of the disputes among impassioned clergymen and their followers, and religious controversy came more and more to appear an obstacle in the way of something much more important – the development and spread of education. The memory of the intensely bitter and determined opposition aroused by the Act of 1902 and the attempts subsequently made to alter its provisions were very long lasting. Fears of disturbing 'the settlement of 1902' and of the delicate balance said to have been then achieved were often felt (and perhaps even more often expressed) by politicians called upon to change the existing arrangements.

Decline of active secularism in the Labour and Socialist movements

One significant feature of the struggle over the education Bills brought in by the Conservatives and Liberals between 1896 and 1906 had been the failure of the secularist campaign conducted by some sections of the Socialist and Labour movements. The Socialist Democratic Federation, founded in 1884, had from its beginnings advocated secularism in the schools, and the Labour Representation Committee, founded in 1900, had worked with it in 1902 to advocate continuance of the school boards, as also the abolition of clerical control of the schools and the giving of religious instruction therein. In general the Labour movement regarded the religious controversy as a disgraceful struggle between the rival creeds for control of the minds of working-class children, and the Act of 1902 seemed to most active members of the movement a deplorable victory for clericalism.

In 1906 the Trades Union Congress put forward a Bill proposing that local education authorities should be empowered to purchase or rent any denominational or private school; if consent was not forthcoming the authority would build a new council school, whereupon the grant to the existing school would cease. In all state-aided schools only secular education would be given and there would be no religious tests for the teachers (Simon, 1965, 257). In December 1906, Keir Hardie, the leader of the new parliamentary Labour party, informed the Commons that the T.U.C., 'with two million affiliated members, had four times in succession declared for a national system of education under popular control, free and secular from primary school to university. The great majority of the members ... were, like himself, Christians, but they supported the secular solution owing to the impossibility of finding a common denominator that all would accept' (ibid., 260). Year after year the Labour Party Conference and the Trades Union Congress voted overwhelmingly in favour of the exclusion of religious education from schools receiving public funds; but growing opposition from some members holding strong religious convictions, particularly from Roman Catholics, gave rise to dissension and threatened to split the working-class movements. The subject was no longer discussed at either meeting from 1913 onwards.

The failure of the Fisher proposals of 1920

One immediate result of the outbreak of the First World War was, of course, a deterioration in educational provision, because of the postponement of building and maintenance, the shortage of teachers, an increase in the size of classes, and so on; but wartime experiences also inspired a certain amount of idealistic hope for a more just and better educated society in the future, together with some realization that further waste of human resources must be avoided. The Workers' Educational Association, the National Union of Teachers, and a number of leading educationalists, such as those who formed the Education Reform Council in 1916, were among those who advocated the extension of education; they usually asked for the provision of secondary education for all children attaining a suitable standard, the raising of the school leaving age, and compulsory part-time education for a period after leaving school. The Labour and Independent Labour parties demanded 'universal, free, compulsory, secondary education, involving the raising of the school-leaving age to 16 and no exemptions for part-time employment' (ibid., 1965, 348). The general diffusion of elementary education among the working classes was making those most ambitious for their children, and those most politically minded, conscious of the need for greater educational opportunities.

There was, therefore, a good deal of support for H. A. L. Fisher's Education Act of 1918, which, among other things, provided for the establishment of central schools and day-continuation schools, and abolished all exemptions from full-time school attendance up to the age of fourteen. Fisher had hoped to make this limited educational advance without disturbing or even discussing the 'settlement of 1902', particularly as, in addition to other difficulties, he was being pressed by some trade union organizations to build a new education system without reference to religious bodies whose disputes could prevent desirable reforms. The denominational authorities, however, made it clear that, so far from extending their educational provision, they were unable to maintain adequately their existing schools at a time of constantly rising costs.

In 1920 Fisher had to recognize that the state could bring about no real advance without the co-operation of the voluntary bodies, and he began by holding conferences with representatives of the Anglicans and the Free Churches. His proposal was that the voluntary schools should be transferred to the local authorities, but that thereafter facilities should be provided in all publicly aided schools for the giving of denominational instruction where parents so desired. Once again it was acknowledged that special arrangements would have to be made for the Roman Catholic authorities, who would reject any plan involving the extinction of schools having a distinctively Roman Catholic 'atmosphere' in return for the possibility of giving denominational instruction to the relatively small numbers of Roman Catholic children in each of thousands of other schools. Many Anglicans welcomed a proposal which would have relieved them of the burden of building and repairing their schools, and which would have led to an extension of their influence to a great number of schools. Anglican schools were constantly being discontinued and it was obvious that many parents were unlikely to put devotion to the Church of England before the possibility of sending their children to superior schools. The *Church Times* proclaimed that a new situation had arisen: 'the old sectarian strife must be forgotten, for the issue has changed. In bygone days it was whether one or other form of Christianity would get the best of a bargain. Now the issue is whether Christianity or secularism shall be the future creed of England' (quoted Cruickshank, 1963, 116).

Some Free Church leaders were inclined to agree; but others, including the veteran Dr Clifford, were not. As in 1870, and again in 1902, it seemed to many Nonconformists that the very difficulties of the Denominationalists demonstrated their lack of public support and their inability to cope with new demands – were they now once again to be rescued by the state just when their end was near? This attitude, together with the opposition of the Roman Catholics and the rejection of the proposals by the National Union of Teachers, made agreement impossible. In Wales even the readiness of the Established Church to surrender its relatively few schools in return for the provision of undenominational instruction in all schools was unavailing, since the teachers remained, apprehensive of religious tests.

The 'Scottish solution' of 1918

The 'settlement of 1902' had in effect laid it down that those religious bodies who wished to retain possession of their schools, to give denominational instruction, and to control the appointment of teachers, must pay for these privileges by providing and structurally maintaining the schools. But it was possible to argue that the ownership of the building (often erected with borrowed money and still unpaid for) and the control of appointments (limited as this was by the local authority's right to disapprove on secular grounds) were of importance only in so far as they ensured denominational instruction in distinctively denominational schools by teachers of the appropriate faith: so long as these objectives were attained legal ownership and control were irrelevant.

In England and Wales most influential Denominationalists, and certainly all the Roman Catholic authorities, rejected this view; yet in Scotland it formed the basis of a peaceful solution to the religious problem, arrived at in 1918. The Roman Catholics had made great efforts to provide schools: in the thirty years from 1880 to 1910, whereas the number of other voluntary schools fell by almost two-thirds, the number of Roman Catholic schools rose by about 75 per cent; and in the latter year, of 286 voluntary denominational schools, 220 were Roman Catholic (calculated from Robertson, 1951, 330). But by 1918 the Roman Catholic schools, in particular, were faced with immense difficulties because of inadequate accommodation and equipment, and inability to pay suitable salaries.

The 'Scottish solution' of 1918 was the result of amicable discussions between the representatives of the state and of the churches, among the latter the Roman Catholic Bishop of Pella, recently appointed by the Pope to be Apostolic Visitor to Scotland. The managers of the existing church schools, or of any established later, were enabled to sell or lease or otherwise transfer their schools to education authorities; or the education authority might itself supply new denominational schools. The authority henceforth would have complete control of the schools, including the appointment and dismissal of teachers, but the existing teachers would retain their posts and any teacher subsequently appointed must be approved of by the denominational body concerned 'in respect of religious belief and character'. An unpaid supervisor was to be appointed for each school (almost always the parish priest or minister) to ensure that efficient religious instruction was given in the school. Administratively, therefore, the 'dual system' came to an end in Scotland, though the schools differed in the denominational instruction they offered. (It may be added here that the arrangement has worked extremely smoothly since its inception. In 1929 the powers and duties of the original *ad hoc* authorities were taken over by education committees elected from town and county councils.)

Could a similar settlement be made in England and Wales? The situations there were different in many ways. There was much less religious indifference in Scotland and much more concern about educational deprivation; the religious minorities were small, they were narrowly localized, and they constituted no threat to the dominant position of the established church; religious and political passions had not been inflamed by generations of bitter dispute and recrimination in the field of education. For almost half a century it had been widely accepted in England and Wales that there was a legal prohibition of denominational instruction in council schools, whereas no such prohibition had existed in Scotland, and one result was that teachers there were much less inclined to resent religious tests for appointment and promotion. In any case, the Roman Catholic authorities in England and Wales could not agree at the time to propose relinquishing the ownership of their schools. In 1931 the Catholic Education Council did decide to campaign for the adoption of the Scottish system in England and Wales, and in the years that followed the claim was in the forefront of Roman Catholic proposals; but with each year that passed the possibility receded, particularly as the National Union of Teachers could not accept a system which would have involved the introduction of denominational instruction into a greatly increased number of publicly owned schools. Indeed the Catholic Education Council in 1943 itself quoted the organ of the N.U.T. as doubting 'whether the Scottish teachers, as a body, would be so ready today as they were thirty years ago to acquiesce in a solution of this kind' (*The Case for Catholic Schools*, 103).

Denominational schools and 'secondary education for all'

Discussing the provisions of the Education Bill of 1902, Morant had written to Balfour,

> I agree with you that voluntary managers will find it a much more expensive business than they at present realise to bring and keep their buildings up to the increasingly heightened standards of the local authority. And possibly there will be some twenty years hence another 'intolerable strain' in that respect (Allen, 1934, 161).

He was certainly right. After the First World War the economic and social forces which had already created difficulties for the denominational schools became immensely stronger. Building costs rose more or less continuously, and sometimes quite unpredictably, whilst many church schools, among them numbers built with the help of state grants prior to 1870, needed to be replaced or extended. Shifts of population gave rise to demands for new denominational schools: this occurred not only when rural workers came to the towns but when there was movement from the centres of these out to the suburbs. Subscriptions often fell away, whether because of diminishing religious fervour, widespread trade depressions and unemployment, the departure of wealthy patrons to other districts, or a growing tendency, especially outside the Roman Catholic community, to accept the council schools not only as better housed but as providing an adequate religious education – and one shown to be reassuringly Protestant by the absence, generally speaking, of Roman Catholic children.

The difficulties seemed particularly burdensome and unjust whenever the state intervened to lay down improved standards of accommodation, hygiene and sanitation. Slum clearance and town planning projects often faced the denominational bodies with considerable expenditure. But the greatest problems were caused by proposals to raise the age of compulsory attendance at school and to extend the range of public education. Fisher's Act of 1918 had given legal sanction for the establishment of central schools, but, as we have seen, attempts to provide a financial framework enabling the voluntary schools to adopt the policy had failed. In 1926 the *Report of the Consultative Committee on the Education of the Adolescent* (the Hadow Report) gave impetus to a movement already under way in many parts of the country when it recommended that 'post-primary education should be made available for all normal children between the ages of 11 and 14 and, as soon as possible, 11 and 15'. In some cases this might be given in 'senior classes' in existing schools (though even here considerable expenditure on alterations and new equipment would be involved); the more desirable course would be to establish 'modern' schools for the children for whom the education given in the existing grammar and junior technical schools would be too academic or otherwise unsuitable. In 1938 the *Report of the Consultative Committee on Secondary Education* (the 'Spens Report') emphasized the principle implied in the earlier report that 'parity of schools in the secondary stage of education is essential' : of particular concern to the managers of voluntary schools was the recommendation that in all forms of secondary education, including the new 'modern' schools, there should be equality in the amenities of new buildings, in the size of classes and (eventually) in the minimum school-leaving age.

The acceptance of the 'reorganization' proposals of the Hadow Report clearly threatened the continued existence of the dual system. For the first time since 1870 the denominational bodies were to be called upon to provide quite quickly a vast amount of new accommodation, but now without building grants payable during a 'period of grace', and at a time when concern for denominational instruction was so much diminished among possible subscribers that the Church of England was building few new schools in any case. Given that the churches could not afford to provide the new facilities, children were likely to have to proceed from denominational primary schools to undenominational council secondary schools or to remain without secondary education. Hitherto the denominational authorities had derived security from the knowledge that for the state to replace the voluntary schools would entail very great expense; but now that new schools would be needed in any case the state might argue that since it had to provide them it might well claim to control them. Moreover it was not now a question of some dramatic and forcible seizure which might be denounced and resisted as intolerable persecution; the new schools could be provided 'to fill up the gaps', as the board schools had been, and the parents left to decide whether they wished to take advantage of the new facilities or to continue to send their children to the existing inferior 'all-age' voluntary schools. The Roman Catholic authorities could rely somewhat more assuredly than could the Anglicans on the refusal of many of the parents to send their children to the new council secondary schools; but even to them the threat appeared very dangerous, for the concern for better secular education for their children had much increased among Roman Catholic parents since the days when Roman Catholic bishops might fairly confidently expect obedience to a virtual injunction against attendance at Oxford and Cambridge.

The Anglicans wavered and were divided. In 1926 the Church Assembly, in an aggressive mood, called for the provision of new denominational schools by local education authorities, the right of entry to new council secondary schools to give denominational instruction, and the creation of regional committees to supervise the religious instruction given in all council schools. In 1927, however, the National Society accepted the recommendations of the Hadow Report and proposed the provision of facilities for denominational instruction in the new council secondary schools to which children from Anglican schools would be transferred. Two years later another Anglican committee produced two reports: one, signed by a majority, advocated the handing over of Anglican schools to local authorities and henceforth devoting greater attention to the provision of training colleges; the other insisted upon the retention of church schools and asked for greater support from the state (Cruickshank, 1963, 126).

The Roman Catholic authorities were anxious to obtain adequate financial help, not merely to meet the new situation but on a permanent basis, so as to ensure the future of Roman Catholic schools. Great protest meetings were organized and parliamentary candidates asked to pledge support; in 1929 the hierarchy published an uncompromising declaration that, whilst it was no part of the normal function of the state to provide education, it should do so, in default of other agencies, on behalf of parents: where parents were poor the state should help but should not interfere with the parents' choice of school or discriminate between schools (quoted Beales, 1950, 388-9).

It was difficult for the political parties to know how to act. The rise of the Labour party (up to 1931) and the continued strength of the Conservative party led to close-fought struggles between them; the Liberal party was in decline; each party, therefore, was particularly anxious to win new votes where it could, and to alienate as few supporters as possible. The Church of England was divided, and many Conservative Anglicans were becoming uncomfortably aware that support for Denominationalism increasingly meant disproportionate assistance for Roman Catholic schools. The strength of the Free Church vote had manifestly declined but was difficult to estimate and might still be formidable, as overt hostility to Roman Catholicism certainly remained in some places. After the creation of the Irish Free State in 1921 the Roman Catholic Church could no longer count on the support of a large group of Irish members of parliament and it needed to strengthen its political influence. Many members of the Labour party were traditionally opposed to clericalism, and Roman Catholic (like Anglican) clergy often reciprocated this hostility, feeling that the party was well on the way towards Communism. Moreover many Labour party members came of Nonconformist stock and had no love for Rome. Yet the party in some areas relied greatly on the support of Roman Catholic workers. An interesting situation developed in Liverpool, 'the English capital of the Roman Church', in 1925, when, with the encouragement of the clergy, a Catholic party was set up to contest local elections, principally in order to safeguard Roman Catholic interests in the sphere of education. The Archbishop of Liverpool asked, 'However well disposed the various political parties may be to our reasonable claims, is it sense to dissipate our enormous voting power among their nominees, when, with a minimum of organization, we can return our own?' The vote of the Roman Catholic working class was split: Roman Catholic priests were to be found contesting seats, not always successfully, against Roman Catholic members of the Labour party. In 1927 the Catholic party was the second largest (after the Conservative) on the town council. But there were manifest dangers to the church from this undisguised entry into the political arena, whether election results were favourable or not, and occasional indiscretions by the clergy gave opportunities for recrimination within and outside its membership, so that in 1928 a new Archbishop (Dr Downey) considered it wise to dissolve the party and forbid priests to take part in elections. Nevertheless the Labour party had been warned that the votes of Roman Catholic workers would have to be earned.

Whilst it was thus made very clear to all political parties that, at a period when religious indifference was growing, well organized groups could exercise a decisive influence, on the other hand the N.U.T. was, as ever, watchful to oppose the wider spread of denominational teaching as the result of government action. Meanwhile educational advance appeared not merely desirable (all the more so since raising the school-leaving age would reduce the great number of potential workers unemployed), but inevitable; it was indeed already in progress in some areas as a consequence of local administrative action in response to the same social pressures as had led to the establishment of higher-grade elementary schools in the previous century.

Attempts by the Labour government of 1929-31 to formulate acceptable policies proved abortive: it had no overall majority and could hardly have hoped to succeed, especially since the House of Lords was opposed to the raising of the school-leaving age and many Roman Catholics among Labour members of parliament refused to accept a temporary solution designed to cope only with the current situation. But the immensely strong 'National' government which followed was eventually able to pass the Education Act of 1936, based partly on proposals which had failed to become law in 1931. It empowered local authorities to make grants of 50 to 75 per cent towards the cost of building voluntary schools made necessary by the state's declared intention to raise the legal school-leaving age to fifteen on 1 September 1939, and to 'reorganize' the educational provision. To meet the demands of Free Churchmen and the N.U.T. this arrangement was to be strictly temporary – proposals had to be submitted within three years; only accommodation for senior children was involved; teachers for the schools receiving building grants would be appointed by the local education authority, though a limited proportion (to be agreed upon by the authority and the school managers) would be 'reserved' teachers, i.e. chosen in consultation with the managers as qualified to give the appropriate denominational instruction. Undenominational religious instruction according to the syllabus prescribed for the local council schools was to be provided in all voluntary schools for children whose parents so desired.

In Liverpool the local Conservatives, true to their by now traditional alliance with the militant Protestants, refused to make the grants provided for in the Act of 1936 towards the building of denominational schools. Feelings ran extremely high and the government had to intervene, in the manner of the heady days following the passing of the Act of 1902, by cutting off part of the annual state grant to the city. A compromise was reached in 1939 with the passing of a special Act of Parliament for Liverpool, empowering the council to build senior schools for renting to denominational bodies.

In general the Anglican authorities felt unable or disinclined to avail themselves of the limited assistance afforded by the 1936 Act. By 1938 they had surrendered many schools to local authorities; in some areas agreements were entered into with the authorities that, in all 'reorganized' schools: (a) children might be withdrawn at arranged times to receive denominational instruction – this was permitted by the Act of 1902; or (b) the clergy or other denominational teachers might be allowed to enter the school to give denominational instruction; or, (c) a syllabus of religious instruction agreed upon by the local Anglicans and Nonconformists might be adopted for the schools. Such compromise solutions allowed some local authorities to make good progress with 'reorganization', but of course many Anglicans refused to countenance these arrangements and the Roman Catholic authorities rejected them outright.

The school-leaving age was not raised on 1 September 1939: the 'appointed day' was also that chosen by Hitler for the start of the Second World War.

8

The Education Act, 1944

The climate of opinion

Whilst the war of 1939-45 was still being fought there was much discussion of the need to build a new society in Britain when it ended. To those who wished to see considerable advances in educational provision, unhindered by religious controversy, the prospects seemed favourable. There was a coalition government; the nation was united in sacrifice and endeavour. Many of those indifferent to religion felt that educational progress was far more important than disputes among the churches, and many others deeply attached to their own branch of Christianity had come to think that, whilst the need for religious education was clearly greater than ever, sectarian differences mattered much less than the need to combat atheistic Communism or pagan Nazism. The results of anti-semitism had shown what evil forces might be released by religious and racial intolerance, and two world wars had made nonsense of genuine doubts or prejudiced claims about the allegiance of Roman Catholics and Jews. Bomb damage, the increased mobility of the population and (later) slum clearance helped to break up some at least of the enclaves of bigotry and intolerance which had affected local, and sometimes national, politics.

The need for action was clear enough. School buildings and maintenance had practically ceased during the war, and many schools had been destroyed; there was a great shortage of teachers; the pre-war plans for raising the school-leaving age and providing secondary education for all children had still to be implemented. Clearly the contribution of the voluntary schools would be sorely needed, and the country was in no mood to object to moderate concessions. True, the Trades Union Congress in 1942 had declared itself opposed to denominational instruction in schools and to the payment of state grants to denominational training colleges; but Roman Catholic and other trade unionists had effectively protested. Generally speaking, it might be said that a candidate for parliament was far more likely to lose votes than to gain them by manifesting hostility to religion: believers would be offended, and even many of those indifferent would consider him guilty of intolerance or bad taste.

The need for action

In 1870 and in 1902, whatever other forces had been at work, sheer necessity had finally obliged and nerved the state to introduce some workable administrative machinery into the educational system, requiring the disputing groups to accept such compromises as the new arrangements made necessary. Between the two world wars, in spite of the failure of the churches and the state to arrive at a comprehensive national agreement, local administrators, as we have seen, had in some areas succeeded in effecting limited concordats making educational 'reorganization' possible. But, generally speaking, the dual system constituted in 1939 an intolerable obstacle to progress. According to a government White Paper published in 1943, the system had engendered friction and had given rise to endless complications in administration. It was 'inconsistent with proper economy and efficiency'. Ninety-two per cent of the voluntary schools were more than forty years old; most of them, and particularly the Anglican schools, were very small. The state could not close a voluntary school of thirty or more pupils (however uneconomic to staff and maintain) unless a school of the same denomination was available, even though there was unused accommodation in a nearby council school. A local authority could not insist on filling a vacancy in a voluntary school by transferring a redundant teacher from another school in its area. Of the children in the relevant age range, 62 per cent of those attending state schools were by March 1939 in senior schools or departments; this was true of only 16 per cent of those attending voluntary schools (*Educational Reconstruction*, 1943, 13).

When R. A. Butler became President of the Board of Education in 1941 he found that yet again the imperative need to find some way out of the existing 'educational muddle' had led administrators of the Board to put forward their own proposals – in a memorandum which became known as the Green Book. (For an account of the proposals and subsequent negotiations see Cruickshank, 1963, 145 ff.) Butler at once agreed upon the necessity for action. It was as clear as it had been in 1870 to most practically minded men that the existence of the voluntary schools could not be ignored, and equally clear both that they would need greater financial assistance and that they must be more closely integrated with the state system.

The policies available

Under the existing law, if the state (or the local authorities under its direction) had assumed complete responsibility for the upkeep and the control of the primary and the new secondary modern schools, the religious instruction given must normally not be denominational; indeed there would be no legal requirement that any religious instruction whatever should be given. Administrators and politicians alike were generally agreed that extended control must not involve the prohibition of denominational teaching. The government's policy was declared in general terms in 1943:

> Discussions carried on in recent months with the many interests concerned have satisfied the Government that there is a wide measure of agreement that voluntary schools should not be abolished but rather that they should be offered further financial assistance, accompanied by a corresponding extension of public control which will ensure the effective and economical organization and development of both primary and secondary education. It is believed that the view will generally be taken that in framing the proposals for such control the services of the churches to the community as pioneers in public education, as the protagonists of Christian teaching in schools and as having for many generations voluntarily spent large sums on the provision and upkeep of premises for this purpose, cannot justly be disregarded (*Educational Reconstruction*, 1943, 14).

There appeared to be three possible ways of effecting the necessary administrative changes whilst making the position acceptable to Denominationalists. The central and local governments might accept complete financial responsibility for the voluntary schools, and in return assume full control, whilst permitting them to be staffed by teachers of the appropriate faith with unrestricted freedom to give denominational instruction – as under the Scottish system. But this could lead to a very wide-spread development of denominational schools by active religious bodies no longer restrained by financial considerations, and for this reason the policy would be opposed not only by Free Churchmen (still especially concerned about single-school areas and religious tests for teachers) and by teachers' organizations, but by all those unwilling to see a great increase in the influence of the churches in the schools. The claim of the Roman Catholic authorities that the state should adopt the solution to 'the religious problem' accepted in Scotland was rejected by the government quite firmly:

> It is clear that the solution must take different lines here and

cannot ignore the principle embodied ... in the 1870 Act and firmly rooted in the convictions of many elements in this country that the State, concerned though it is to ensure a sound religious basis for all education, cannot take on itself the full responsibility for fostering the teaching of formularies distinctive of particular denominations designed to attach children to particular worshipping communities (ibid., 15).

In practice, therefore, two lines of policy in regard to the voluntary schools remained open to the state: complete financial support (involving more or less complete control) with limited facilities accorded for denominational instruction; or limited financial support and control, with practically unrestricted facilities for denominational instruction. The former arrangement naturally had most appeal for administrators and for those Anglican authorities finding it almost impossible to maintain their schools: the latter for some other Anglicans and for the Roman Catholics. The state decided to adopt both plans.

The problems likely to ensue from this decision were obvious. If too much freedom to give denominational instruction were permitted under the first scheme, or too much financial support under the second, there would not only be criticism from the traditional sources but a sense of grievance among those who, for financial or conscientious reasons, had chosen what had become the least favoured policy. Moreover, past events had shown clearly enough that to accept conscientious insistence upon denominational instruction as valid, yet justifying the grant of only fixed and limited financial support, was to make future educational progress largely dependent on the willingness and ability of one part of the population to make a disproportionate contribution towards it.

The rival interests

The difficulties of R. A. Butler, as representing the state, in negotiating the new 'settlement' have been more than a little exaggerated. The discussions were necessarily lengthy and called for both firmness and tact. It was, of course, a necessary part of his strategy to persuade all concerned that only the utmost willingness to compromise could preserve a delicate balance of forces and prevent disastrous consequences. But he occupied a position of great strength, and to speak in terms more appropriate to the situation in 1902 is misleading. He was not attempting to destroy the existing dual system but to augment and reinforce it. If accused of extending state control he could point to the alternative arrangements available. He was able to demonstrate to the Archbishop of Canterbury (Cruickshank, 1963, 151-2) that the Anglican church was in no position to finance the improvements needed in its schools – and indeed it could not be denied that the Anglican contribution to the national provision of education had much diminished since the turn of the century (see below, chapter 9); as we have seen, not only were many Anglican schools very small and uneconomic to run but they were often located where they were no longer needed, and yet there had been little provision of new schools for decades. Membership of the church and financial support had much declined. But the most fundamental weakness of the Anglican position has already been referred to: the religious instruction provided in council schools, minimal though it often was, satisfied the desire of most of the parents concerned to have their children given such religious instruction as would, it was hoped, improve character and conduct.

The Roman Catholic authorities, on the other hand, could point to continued successful efforts to augment educational provision and to the conscientious support of a strong body of parents (and voters) determined to have their children taught Roman Catholic doctrine by Roman Catholic teachers; however, partly because of their relative success, the Roman Catholic hierarchy could no longer rely on the political support of the Anglican church – or even on that of some of their own followers, since social considerations and class or political solidarity now often carried more weight than the advice or instructions of church leaders. But in any case what the state was offering to the Roman Catholic authorities was improved financial support; they might protest that it was, and would increasingly prove to be, inadequate, but they could hardly refuse to accept it.

Of the other interested parties, Free Churchmen had not been able at the height of their political power decades earlier to prevent the establishment or continuance of the dual system: they were hardly likely to succeed now, especially since their traditional demand that denominational instruction be left to the parents or the Sunday schools was becoming ever more unrealistic, as many of them were well aware. As for the teachers, whatever their leaders might say, fears of clerical supervision had receded and statutory guarantees against victimization on religious grounds in regard to appointment and promotion were now largely taken for granted – and were by no means always considered to be effective in the case of the latter. In any event one of the arrangements proposed by the state would involve a reduction in the number of teachers appointed on religious grounds to the staffs of some schools formerly denominational.

In effect a Conservative minister had once again intervened to ensure the continuance of the dual system: even if R. A. Butler had been personally disposed to adopt harsh policies towards the Anglican church he would not have been free to do so, for, as we have seen, there was a long established tradition within the Conservative party of combining firm talk to archbishops with some attachment to the church and acceptance of it as a considerably junior but nevertheless valuable partner of the state, and a bulwark against subversion. He could not have gone far without incurring the severe displeasure of influential groups within his party. But then it is difficult to imagine that a representative of either of the other parties could have taken a substantially different line in the circumstances which history had brought about.

Except, perhaps, in one respect : the decision (made at the joint request of Anglican and Free Church leaders) to make religious instruction and a daily 'act of corporate worship' compulsory in all primary and secondary schools assisted from public funds. Scarcely any managers of such schools were at this time availing themselves of the freedom allowed since 1870 to dispense with religious instruction, and the new declaration of principle gave rise to surprisingly little comment, except from some teachers' representatives who considered it unnecessary. Yet it clearly indicated a desire for closer co-operation between church and state, and seemed to signal the end of the long struggle to confine state-supported education to secular subjects. But its influence was more than symbolic : henceforward religious instruction in council schools would be, generally speaking, greater in extent and more systematic; moreover, since the daily act of worship would in practice normally be conducted by the head teacher, this lent support, as we shall see, to the contention of those who felt that, whatever the 1944 Act might elsewhere prescribe, head teachers should be chosen from among committed Christians. The implications could hardly be inconsiderable.

Provisions for religious instruction

The other provisions of the Act of 1944 relating to religious instruction may be summarized as follows :

1   In *all* primary and secondary schools assisted from public funds not only would the right of withdrawal be preserved but children so withdrawn might be given religious instruction in accordance with parental wishes if this could reasonably be arranged. The requirement of the Education Act of 1902 that times for religious instruction should be 'conveniently arranged' to facilitate withdrawal would be abolished, so that greater use could be made of those teachers willing and able to give the instruction.

2 In secondary and primary schools *wholly* maintained from public funds the provision of religious instruction and a daily 'act of corporate worship' would be compulsory, though no teacher might legally be compelled to take part, or refused employment or promotion for doing so or not doing so. The instruction must not be 'distinctive of any particular religious denomination' and must in each locality be in accordance with a syllabus unanimously agreed upon by a committee representing the local education authority, the Church of England (except in Wales), and such other religious denominations as the authority considered appropriate.

3 The state agreed to provide financial support for three categories of primary and secondary denominational schools; in all of them the whole cost of the secular and religious instruction would come from public funds, the state reserving the right to ensure that the schools were needed and that new ones were established only as national resources permitted. The three categories were to be:

i Voluntary aided schools These would be fully denominational, the voluntary bodies having the same rights as hitherto concerning the giving of denominational religious instruction, the appointment of teachers, and the nomination of two-thirds of the managers. But the state now agreed

(a) to pay to the managers of all voluntary aided schools 50 per cent of approved expenditure on repairs and improvements required to keep the schools up to the necessary standard, and

(b) to pay up to 50 per cent of the cost of alterations made necessary by the decision to provide secondary education for all up to the age of at least fifteen ('reorganization'). This latter concession clearly paved the way for the re-introduction, after more than sixty years, of building grants, since it would sometimes be cheaper to build a new school than to alter an old one.

The state therefore undertook, in carefully defined circumstances, to pay up to 50 per cent of the cost of providing certain voluntary aided schools. Broadly speaking, this was where it was necessary to build the schools as a result of 'reorganization', or where slum clearance or town planning legislation made necessary the 'displacement' of children and the establishment of new schools. (Since only a proportion of children attending a new school might have been 'displaced' in this way, and the grant was estimated accordingly, the possibilities of dispute were almost limitless.) Loans on favourable terms would normally be made available to managers of voluntary aided schools to help them to meet their obligations, and accommodation for ancillary services (medical inspection, school meals, etc.) would be paid for by the state.

ii Special agreement schools In practice these would be much the same as voluntary aided schools. As we have seen, the state had empowered local authorities in 1936 to make grants of 50 to 75 per cent of the cost of building new denominational secondary schools, proposals to be submitted within three years. Only 519 proposals had in fact been made (289 of them in respect of Roman Catholic schools) and only thirty-seven schools were built before the outbreak of the Second World War. The state now agreed that proposals made under the Act of 1936 could be revived (with any necessary modifications) on the conditions formerly laid down limiting the number of teachers appointed as qualified to give denominational teaching. The provisions regarding the proportion of managers representing the denominational authority, and the grants and loans available towards the cost of improvements and external repairs, would be as for voluntary aided schools.

iii Controlled schools Where a denominational body, in spite of the additional state assistance now offered, felt unable or unwilling to undertake to pay its share of the cost of necessary improvements and repairs, the state offered an arrangement designed to mitigate the effect of complete surrender of the premises. The church authorities would in principle retain ownership of the school but would appoint only one-third of the managers, and the school would be financed and maintained exactly as if it were a council school. There would, however, be two concessions in return for the surrender of the school:

(*a*) although religious instruction would normally be undenominational and according to the local 'agreed syllabus' (as in council schools), denominational instruction might be given in accordance with previous practice on not more than two occasions each week, where parents so desired;

(*b*) to make this possible a carefully defined small proportion of 'reserved' teachers 'selected for their fitness and competence to give such religious instruction' could be appointed in schools having more than two teachers; in small controlled schools, however, the denominational teaching might be given by any non-reserved teacher who volunteered, or by anyone else – including a clergyman – approved by the managers connected with the denomination concerned. All teachers were to be appointed by the local education authority: in an attempt to satisfy the conflicting views of teachers' organizations and the different church authorities, it was provided that head teachers would not be 'reserved', though the denominational body would be allowed to express its views about any head teacher whom it was proposed to appoint.

It may be noted that controlled status involved arrangements very similar to the version of the Irish System which the Roman

Catholics had accepted in the Liverpool Corporation Schools (1836-42), and which the Church of England had denounced with such vigour when Lord John Russell had made the state's first tentative attempt to deal with the religious problem with the proposed establishment of a training college and model school in 1839. The distinction between 'voluntary aided' and 'controlled' status also had an obvious affinity with Birrell's proposals of 1906 providing for 'extended' and 'ordinary' facilities for denominational instruction.

The reactions of the churches

The attitudes of the Anglican authorities towards the new arrangements varied. The Church of England Council for Education, in a report published in 1954 (*The Church and the Schools*), explained:

> Many Churchmen believed that in this new [i.e. controlled] type of school a solution had been found for many of the Church's educational problems. It was felt that the State was being very generous in relieving [the Church] of financial responsibility for the buildings and it was thought that what the Church surrendered in control would, through the goodwill of the [local] Authorities, make little difference to the character of the school. Other Churchmen believed that controlled status was not worth having and applauded the decision of the Roman Catholic Education Council to have nothing to do with this type of school.

Of course controlled status was often accepted only because of the difficulty of raising large sums of money in a short time for repairs, alterations or even new building. Since a considerable part of the time available for religious instruction in controlled schools could still be devoted to specifically Anglican beliefs, what was at stake was the distinctly Anglican 'atmosphere' of the school. However, the new arrangement appeared to guarantee the continuance of Anglican teaching for the foreseeable future in what would otherwise become undenominational council schools.

The Roman Catholics in 1944 rejected controlled status completely (though, apparently as the result of an administrative oversight, two very small Roman Catholic school departments were in fact accorded controlled status). Throughout the negotiations leading up to the 1944 Act the Roman Catholic authorities had insisted that, in justice, they were entitled to 100 per cent support for the provision and maintenance of their schools, but that, to meet the objections of others, they would settle for the 'Scottish solution', surrendering their schools if the state undertook to maintain existing schools and to provide new ones as required, there being guarantees as to the appointment of Roman Catholic teachers.

Failing that, they would accept an arrangement similar to that arrived at in Liverpool in 1939, whereby new schools would be built by the local authority and rented to the school managers. When both of these proposals were rejected they demanded that the grant for alterations and improvements be raised to 75 per cent and that the same grant be payable towards the cost of *all* new schools, not merely those needed for 'displaced' pupils. When this also was refused they asked for an assurance that if building costs after the war rose more than the 35 per cent over 1939 prices which the government had predicted they should be reimbursed for the extra expense entailed in building schools. This assurance was not given.

The Act of 1944 was the result of prolonged negotiations between the President of the Board of Education and representatives of the Anglicans, the Free Churches, the Roman Catholics and the teachers. Of these only the Roman Catholics remained hostile to the end: since controlled status was unacceptable to them they faced an immense task in financing an educational programme in extremely difficult conditions. Associations of Roman Catholic 'parents and electors' had been formed from 1942 onwards and a remarkable campaign of organized opposition to the state's proposals was mounted, but with little immediate result. A revival of the campaign, designed to draw pledges from parliamentary candidates in 1950, failed in its effect, largely because no political party was inclined to re-open the controversial issue. But in 1953 the government was induced to widen the definition of 'displaced pupil' in a way favourable to denominational bodies building schools in new housing areas; to balance this, provision was made for the establishment of new controlled schools, where necessary, in replacement of old.

The concessions of 1959

It soon became obvious that the burden of the Anglicans and Roman Catholics in trying to provide new secondary schools was beyond their strength. The Roman Catholics began in 1956 to prepare for further claims on state assistance; they made approaches in the following years to representatives of the Anglicans, the Free Churches, the teachers and Members of Parliament, as well as to responsible Ministers of the government. Their claim was for 'a grant out of public funds on all approved voluntary school building' (Beck, 1959, 16). The Labour M.P.s were informed that 'The Bishops would look upon a flat grant of 75 per cent as a long term settlement' of the problem, whilst Mr Butler, now Home Secretary, was told in 1958 that an increase in the amount of grant merely for reorganisation would not be sufficient for our needs. It was imperative to have some assistance for the building of new schools, and if we got a grant for new schools the question of voluntary schools' finance would be taken out of politics for twenty years. If it was refused we should find ourselves obliged to come back again with further requests in within five or six years.

Mr Butler was surprised to be informed by Bishop Beck that 'about 30 per cent' of the Roman Catholic children of school age were not in Roman Catholic schools (ibid., 11, 12). The Bishop had indicated in 1947 that the proportion was then one in four, as compared with one in five just before the Second World War (*Case for Catholic Schools*, 1955, 27).

Since the Church of England authorities had considerably lightened their financial commitments by accepting controlled status for many of their schools, many Anglican leaders were less inclined to claim increased assistance for building new schools. The Roman Catholic negotiators felt that the representatives of the Free Churches and of the Church of England were concerned about the assistance which the extension of building grants would give to the Roman Catholics; it was considered that 'most of this opposition' came from the Anglicans, who seemed disturbed by the prospect of a big increase in the Roman Catholic school population as the result of the higher Roman Catholic birth rate (ibid., 19). For whatever reason, the Anglicans pressed only for an increase in the grants for maintenance and improvements. Nevertheless the Education Act of 1959, besides increasing the grants formerly payable from fifty to seventy-five per cent, provided for seventy-five per cent grants for the building of new voluntary secondary schools needed wholly or mainly to cope with children from those primary schools of the same denomination which existed on 15 June 1959 (or from primary schools built to replace those then existing). The limitation imposed by the date, and by the exclusion of grants for building primary, secondary grammar and technical schools, naturally disappointed the Roman Catholics. The state appeared determined to preserve a balance between the opposing claims, making clear that the departure from principle involved in making building grants was, in theory at any rate, a temporary measure to deal with a specific situation. The 'religious problem' remained unsolved.

9

The end of 'passionate intensity'?

Changing attitudes in the Free Churches

But during the 1960s controversy about the relations between church and state in the field of education continued to diminish. The constant decline in dogmatic religious belief made most of the old arguments appear irrelevant to many people, and indeed some new formulations of belief could well make an Anglican, for instance, feel that he had more in common with a Free Church-man or even a Roman Catholic than with one of his own bishops. The ecumenical movement, though it proceeded much more slowly than some wished, at least arose from recognition of the need of the churches to combat secularism together and lowered the temperature of discussion. Old grievances were seen to have become less important or to have virtually disappeared: when Free Church leaders claimed in 1959 that there might be 200 or 300 single-school areas, the Minister for Education pointed out that in 1944 there had been 'some 4,000'. He added that neither the Church of England nor the state would be likely to encourage the establishment of new denominational schools where this would create new single-school areas (*Hansard*, 608, cols. 488, 494, 495, 498).

The state's concessions to the Denominationalists in 1959 made a considerable impression on many Free Churchmen. A pamphlet issued by the Free Church Federal Council observed:

It is certain that the year 1959 has marked a definite change in the nature of the education problem.... The Free Churches saw that their ideal of non-sectarian Christian education for all children would never become acceptable to either Roman Catholics or Anglicans. And Christians of every church recognised with great anxiety that increasing numbers of children are growing up with no real contact with a church of any kind ... the great majority of English people ... live like pagans, belonging to no worshipping community, though perhaps vaguely considering themselves to be Christians. Fifty years ago the situation was not nearly so grave as it is today ... it could reasonably be hoped that non-sectarian Christian teaching in day-school would be followed by active linking with a worshipping community through home, Sunday School or Church. That is no longer true. The Roman Catholics and the Anglicans are quite justified in being anxious about the education of their own and other children, and Free Churchmen must face the situation as it now is (*Free Church Federal Council Education Policy Committees*, 1959, 1).

In 1959 the Free Church Federal Council, at the suggestion of the state, set up an Education Policy Committee; a similar committee representing the Church of England met with it and thus was formed the Central Joint Education Policy Committee of the Church of England and the Free Church Federal Council. Similar joint committees were established on a regional basis to deal with local problems. The Church of England even agreed that, where appropriate, the Free Churches would be allowed representation on the boards of management of its aided or special agreement schools in single-school areas. In 1961 a *Statement of Educational Policy Adopted by the Methodist Conference* acknowledged that denominational schools were an integral part of the existing educational system (though it felt that the state should make no increase of grant for the maintenance or provision of such schools). Remarking that 'the old causes of friction have almost disappeared', it noted that in some places 'a Church of England voluntary school and a Methodist voluntary school' had combined to form 'one Church of England and Methodist Joint Voluntary Controlled School', and it commended 'such experiments in co-operation' as 'a practical development of partnership in religious education'.

The teachers

After the Nonconformists, the second great traditional source of opposition to unconditional state assistance for denominational schools has been the major organizations of teachers; but, here again, critical attitudes have weakened. In general, teachers, as we have seen, far from opposing the giving of religious instruction in schools, had thought of it as essential and likely to raise their status. As late as 1944 they had opposed the introduction of compulsion only on the grounds that this was both unnecessary and humiliating. Yet the hostility to religious tests had once been widespread. Times are changing, however. There are now fewer fully denominational Anglican schools. The influence exerted in schools by clergymen and members of religious orders is constantly declining. Denominational bodies, though they have won the right to receive considerable public aid whilst retaining the power to appoint teachers of a particular faith, now in practice often consider themselves fortunate to obtain a teacher or lecturer of any religion or of none: this is due not only to the overall shortage of teachers but to the decline in religious loyalties and to the greater inducements to change posts in search of payments for extra responsibilities.

Though teachers' organizations have continued to insist, wherever possible and appropriate, on legal protection from religious tests, the importance of this has declined. Religious instruction is often given by specialists; and, in any case, there is less belief than once there was either in the ability of children to grasp fine doctrinal points or in the value of merely learning by heart the phrases in which these are formulated. The demands made even of a professed believer are often minimal and such as many others would consider it illiberal to reject: unwisely illiberal, at that, since those who appoint to higher posts in schools and colleges of education, even where these are not denominational, are often disinclined to select professed non-Christians, whatever the legal enactments may prescribe. Thus a leading article in *The Times Educational Supplement* has claimed (24 April 1964) that in view of the state's decision in 1944 to make religious instruction and worship compulsory in schools aided from public funds,

> ... one can hardly criticize ... the practice of appointing bodies in choosing invariably [*sic*] Christian men and women as heads of schools.... This may appear rather hard on agnostics who enjoy promotion no less than other men and are strongly enough represented in the schools to lay claim to more headships than they probably possess. All the same, the climate in which he is going to work is in no way concealed from the agnostic when he enters the teaching profession of his own free will; the close historical connection between religion and education in Britain existed for centuries before the Act of 1944.

More remarkable than the somewhat selective respect for the provisions of the 1944 Act here displayed is the fact that this assertion in the most read educational journal in the kingdom, which would have aroused such a storm even twenty years earlier, created no stir whatever.

The Education Act, 1967

In 1964 the Labour party came to power committed to yet another reorganization of the educational system (already begun in some areas), with a view to discontinuing the segregation of children according to ability in schools of different types. Since this 'comprehensive' plan would eventually entail the provision of great numbers of new and larger schools, the denominational bodies were naturally concerned, and the Roman Catholic authorities, in particular, made it clear that, although they were not opposed in principle to the new policy, they would expect the state to ensure that they 'were not financially worse off if they decided to fall in with the scheme' (*T.E.S.*, 8 May 1964, 1250). But the state now needed little convincing of the necessity and practicability of providing further assistance to meet the current and future educational commitments of the churches. In February 1966 a government spokesman announced that, with the approval of all three parties in parliament and of the religious bodies concerned, the state would undertake not merely to raise to eighty per cent the existing grant payable to all voluntary aided and special agreement schools for approved repairs and improvements but, much more important, to pay eighty per cent of the cost of establishing 'completely new schools, or enlargements of existing schools' even where these had not hitherto been eligible for such a grant. What appeared to be the amendment of an existing Act was in effect the inauguration of an important new policy, since building grants, whose abolition had been decreed in the Act of 1870, were now to become permanently and generally available for primary, secondary and technical schools, on a much more generous scale than ever before. The spokesman pointed out that the proposed grants fell short of what the churches had asked for: 'most Roman Catholics had wanted 85 per cent, but this would have inevitably called into question ... the whole distinction between the controlled and the voluntary-aid school'. He added, 'No one wants to reopen this major question now' (*Hansard*, 724, cols. 918, 923). The proposals were sanctioned by parliament in 1967 with scarcely a dissentient voice.

Denominational and public authorities and modern education

By this time the long decline in the numbers of children attending Anglican schools, which had begun about 1890, had become very marked. The table shows the percentages of children on the rolls of schools in England and Wales at different periods. (Here, as elsewhere in this book, the numbers in independent, direct grant, nursery and special schools are omitted. The figures, like those given later, are calculated from statistical returns published annually by the Board of Education, the Ministry of Education or the Department of Education & Science.)

Type of School	1900	1938	1962	1967
Council	47·0	69·6	77·6	76·9
Church of England	40·2	22·1	11·9	11·8
Roman Catholic	5·4	7·4	8·4	9·3
Other	7·4	0·9	2·1	2·0

Moreover, although in some areas the Anglican authorities have striven energetically and successfully to retain voluntary aided status for their schools, far more than half of the Anglican schools are now controlled; in many of these the religious instruction differs little or not at all from that given in council schools, and even where advantage is taken of the provisions of the Act of 1944 such schools are, of course, not in the full sense denominational. By 1962, when it was estimated that baptized Roman Catholics constituted about one-eighth or one-ninth of the population, there were (roughly speaking) three children in Roman Catholic schools to every two in fully denominational Anglican schools. The limited state grants were being spent mainly on Roman Catholic schools: the building programmes authorized by the state from 1945 to 1968 (inclusive) were expected to provide two places in Roman Catholic schools for every one in an Anglican school, the proportions being more than three to one if only fully denominational schools are considered.

Of the students in colleges of education in 1963-4 about one-fifth were in colleges connected with the Church of England and about one-tenth in colleges organized by the Roman Catholic church; a small proportion were in colleges run by Methodists, the Free Churches, and undenominational organizations; but more than three-fifths were in colleges wholly maintained and controlled by public authorities. Of the students who began training for teaching in 1964 about one-seventh were in the departments of education of universities, and these are undenominational. In 1967 there were in England and Wales fifty-three colleges of education controlled by voluntary bodies, thirty university departments of education and 128 institutions controlled by local education authorities (the figures include twelve centres for teachers of art and five departments of education in technical colleges).

Public funds are used in other ways to make possible the provision of religious education. Instruction in theology and other aspects of religion is frequently made available at public expense in universities, publicly controlled colleges of education, etc., whilst courses on the methods of religious instruction are provided for students and serving teachers. Maintenance grants may be paid to clergy and members of religious orders attending universities and other educational institutions and to students studying to become ministers of religion.

It would appear that the possibilities of collaboration between church and state are greater now than at any time during the period we have been studying. The churches have established a good deal of harmony among themselves and so made it easier for governments to give the assistance which, it is almost universally recognized, will increasingly be required.

New views on old policies

Yet it can hardly be said that the churches are satisfied with the outcome. For one thing, especially since 1870 it has been true that what went on in schools (as Gladstone had to learn) might be very different from what was decided by church or state or even both together. Thus in 1960 a joint education committee of the Anglican and Free Churches declared that one of the causes of the 'spiritual illiteracy of many secondary school children' was the 'mistaken idea' that the state forbids 'the teaching of Christian doctrine' (as distinct from 'denominational teaching') in council schools; this was said to lead some teachers to impart 'an emasculated kind of religion' and 'to limit their teaching to the historical and ethical' (*Christian Teaching in Schools*, 3). Again, in 1954 the Church of England Council for Education complained that though in many controlled schools the results of religious education were good, many parents, some members of local education authorities and even some clergymen appeared not to realize that these were still '*Church* schools'; in some, 'church teaching' had ceased altogether because parents had not been given forms for requesting such teaching (*The Church and the Schools*, 5).

Moreover it can hardly be denied that agreement has been reached partly because the matters at issue have ceased to seem important to many of those formerly involved, or because old declarations of principle have been given new meanings and only thus become acceptable.

One Anglican bishop declared in 1965 that, because of public indifference, the state's requirement that religious instruction must be provided in primary and secondary schools supported from public funds would 'scarcely survive the next major reform' (*New Statesman*, 9 April 1965). Yet in 1968 Mr Short, Minister for Education and Science (and himself formerly a headmaster), announced his intention to retain in the new Education Bill being prepared the compulsory provisions of the Act of 1944: he felt there was evidence that most people would wish this. But his estimate of the rôle of 'the Religious Education teacher' would have surprised many earlier speakers on this theme:

He does not set out to arouse faith – though that may follow. He does not attempt to use his advantage in the classroom situation to violate the integrity of the child as an individual with an inalienable right to choose what he believes. To do so would be completely unchristian. Nevertheless he must make assumptions – including that of the existence of God. I would not regard this as indoctrination provided the teaching remains honest and open throughout school life and the opportunity to question those assumptions honestly and overtly remains.

The authors of an opinion survey referred to by the Minister in support of his decision on compulsion have written in reply to critics:

The survey appears at one point to suggest to respondents that Religious Education exists to help pupils to become convinced Christians. Secular humanists are always asserting this. An occasional statement in a few agreed syllabuses might suggest this, but any practising teacher could tell them that this is a dead duck today.

Instead, it appears, what is sought is '"open" R.E. for our children, and with a mainly Christian basis' (*T.E.S.*, 2 May 1969). These statements about what is being, or what should be, done in the schools would be contradicted by many in a position to judge: for instance a *Statement of Methodist Educational Policy* in 1961 welcomed what it called 'the trend in recent revisions of agreed syllabuses to provide positive teaching of Christian doctrine'. Nevertheless the Minister's declaration was received calmly (except by those opposed to compulsion), and indeed was warmly welcomed by the largest of the teachers' organizations in Scotland, whilst the corresponding association in England and Wales, the National Union of Teachers, dissented only to the extent of proposing that children of sixteen and over might be excused at their own request from attendance for religious instruction.

A good deal of opposition – apparently far more than the Minister expected – was voiced by secularist organizations and many individuals, including some committed Christians, to the inclusion in any future Act of the provisions relating to compulsory religious instruction contained in the Education Act of 1944. Doubts were expressed whether those relying on the evidence of opinion polls to demonstrate parents' feelings had sufficiently differentiated between the desire to have children taught *about* religion and the wish to have conveyed to them definite religious convictions. A poll conducted in 1969 for the Humanist Association appeared to show that parents were far more concerned about moral instruction than about religious teaching, but it may be doubted whether most are in fact convinced that these can be separated, since some modern philosophical discussions of the subject are unlikely to have come their way and the contrary belief is so frequently stated and implied.

Also important is the growing criticism of the methods hitherto often adopted for religious instruction. For example it is sometimes claimed that, in comparison with modern procedures based on encouraging children to make 'discoveries', dogmatic religious teaching is relatively unsuccessful and unattractive; whilst emphasis on the desirability of integrating subjects in the curriculum has revived on pedagogical grounds a doctrine long advocated as a theological principle, and has caused to appear unsatisfactory or impractical legal 'settlements' requiring the separation of religious and secular instruction (as for example where the right to withdraw from religious instruction is at issue).

Moreover there is growing doubt whether the results of denominational instruction justify the financial sacrifice and the social segregation entailed. Many Anglicans, as we have seen, have welcomed controlled school status and co-operation with Free Churchmen. Even in Roman Catholic circles in various parts of the world, including the United States, England and Scotland (Spencer, 1968, 166-7), there is now some uncertainty about policies which in Britain have appeared sacrosanct for well over a century. In a recent symposium by Roman Catholic writers, A. E. C. W. Spencer produced evidence purporting to show that in England (as A. M. Greeley and Peter H. Rossi had sought to demonstrate in the United States) attendance at a Roman Catholic school has less influence on subsequent continued religious observance than has the influence of the home; he concluded that 'the empirical basis of the strategy of providing a place in a Catholic school for all Catholic children is extremely doubtful' (ibid., 207). A Roman Catholic priest has pointed to such precedents as the 'Liverpool experiment' of 1836-42 as demonstrating that experiments in sharing Christian schools with other denominations would be within Roman Catholic educational tradition (Gaine, 1968, 163). Among those Roman Catholics advocating a less rigid attitude than hitherto have been Professor A. C. F. Beales, who earlier played a leading part in the campaign for greater state assistance for Roman Catholic schools, and the International Committee of the Newman Association which, in *Reflections on Education*, has proposed reducing the burden of providing denominational instruction by 'not seeking to go beyond the primary stage of education, by coming to arrangements for shared secondary schools – and some primary schools – with other Christian bodies; or by seeking more positive arrangements for the provision of Catholic instruction within the State system'. Such views are far from being officially accepted, but the loyalty and good faith of those who express them is not questioned.

A century after the passing of the Elementary Education Act of 1870 the state is more willing than ever before to assist the churches in the field of education, and in Great Britain, though certainly not in Northern Ireland, the old bitterness of religious controversy has almost faded away. Those who took part in the conflicts earlier described, if they could survey the modern scene, would no doubt assume that in most parts of the field the long battle was ending: though another dispute might well begin about who had won or what the consequences of victory would be. At the end of it all the climate of opinion evinces so relatively little of what used to be called 'religious concern' that there is hesitation and doubt in church circles about future policies; and it may be that in the next hundred years the problems for the churches in educational work will be such as cannot be solved by assistance, however generous, from the state.

Select bibliography

(Published in London unless otherwise stated; standard histories of education are omitted)

(Published in London unless otherwise stated)

ADAMS, F., *History of the Elementary School Contest in England*, 1882.

AKENSON, D. H., *The Irish Education Experiment: The National System of Education in the Nineteenth Century*, Routledge & Kegan Paul, 1970.

ALLEN, B. M., *Sir Robert Morant*, Macmillan, 1934.

AMERY, J., *The Life of Joseph Chamberlain*, Macmillan, Vol. IV, 1951.

ARMSTRONG, R. A., *Henry William Crosskey, his Life and Work*, Birmingham 1895.

ARMYTAGE, W. H. G., *A. J. Mundella, 1825-1897*, Benn, 1951.

ARMYTAGE, W. H. G., *The American Inflence on English Education*, Routledge & Kegan Paul, 1967.

ARNOLD, M., *Schools and Universities on the Continent*, 1868.

AUCHMUTY, J. J., *Irish Education: A Historical Survey*, Harrap, 1937.

AUCHMUTY, J. J., *Sir Thomas Wyse, 1791-1862*, King, 1939.

BAINES, E., *Education Best Promoted by Perfect Freedom, not by State Endowments*, 1854.

BAINES, E., *Letters to the Rt. Hon. Lord John Russell on State Education*, 1846.

BAINES, E., *National Education: Address ... at Manchester ... October 11th, 1867*, 1867.

BAINES, E., *National Education Union, Opening Address at the Educational Conference held at Leeds December 8th, 1869*, 1870.

BALL, N., *Her Majesty's Inspectorate 1839-1849*, University of Birmingham, 1963.

BARKER, E., *Political Thought in England, 1848-1914*, O.U.P., 1945.

BATTERBERRY, R. P. J., *Sir Thomas Wyse, 1791-1862*, Dublin, 1939.

BEALES, A. C. F., 'The Free Churches and the Catholic Schools,' *The Month*, 179, November-December, 1943.

BEALES, A. C. F., 'The Scottish Solution in England and Wales,' *The Month*, 179, March-April, 1943.

BEALES, A. C. F., 'The Struggle for the Schools' in Beck, G. A. (ed.), *The English Catholics 1850-1950*, Burns Oates, 1950.

BECK, G. A., 'Background to the Education Act, 1959'. *Catholic Education*, No. 7, 1959.

130

BECK, G. A., 'The Cost of the Schools', *Clergy Review*, January 1955.

BECK, G. A. (ed.), *The English Catholics 1850-1950*, Burns Oates, 1950.

BELL, G. K. A., *Randall Davidson*, 2 vols., O.U.P., 3rd ed., 1952.

BEST, G. F. A., *Temporal Pillars*, C.U.P., 1964.

BEST, G. F. A., 'The Constitutional Revolution 1828-1832 and its Consequences for the Established Church', *Theology*, LXII, 1959.

BEST, G. F. A., 'The Religious Difficulties of National Education in England, 1800-1870', *Cambridge Historical Journal*, XII, 2, 1956.

BEST, G. F. A., 'The Whigs and the Church Establishment in the Age of Grey and Holland', *History*, XLV, 1960.

BIBER, J., *Bishop Blomfield and his Times*, 1857.

BINGHAM, J. H., *The Period of the Sheffield School Board 1870-1903*, Northend, Sheffield, 1949.

BINNS, H. B., *A Century of Education, Being the Centenary History of the British and Foreign School Society 1808-1908*, Dent, 1908.

BLOMFIELD, A. (ed.), *A Memoir of Charles James Blomfield ... with Selections from his Correspondence*, 2 vols., 1863.

BOOTH, C., *Life and Labour of the People in London*, Third Series, Macmillan, 1902.

BOWEN, D., *The Idea of the Victorian Church*, McGill University Press, Montreal, 1968.

BRENNAN, E. J. T., *The Influence of Sidney and Beatrice Webb on English Education* (unpublished M.A. thesis, University of Sheffield), 1959.

BRIGHT, J., and ROGERS, J. E. J. (ed.), *Speeches on Questions of Public Policy by Richard Cobden, M.P.*, 2 vols., 1870.

BROUGHAM, H., *A Letter on National Education to the Duke of Bedford*, 1839.

BROUGHAM, H., *Speeches of Henry, Lord Brougham*, 4 vols., Edinburgh, 1838.

BROWN, C. K. F., *The Church's Part in Education 1833-1941 with Special Reference to the Work of the National Society*, National Society, 1942.

BURGESS, H. J., *Enterprise in Education, the Story of the Work of the Established Church in the Education of the People prior to 1870*, National Society, 1958.

BURKE, T., *Catholic History of Liverpool*, Tinling, Liverpool, 1910.

BUTLER, E. C., *The Life and Times of Bishop Ullathorne, 1806-1889*, 2 vols., Burns Oates, 1926.

CANNON, C., 'The Influence of Religion on Educational Policy 1902-1944', *British Journal of Educational Studies*, XII, 2, May 1964.

CARLILE, J., *Defence of the National System of Education in Ireland*, 1838.

CARR, J. A., *The Life-Work of Edward White Benson*, 1898.

CHADWICK, O., *The Victorian Church*, Black, 1966.

CLARKE, F., and others, *Church Community and State in Relation to Education*, Allen & Unwin, 1938.

COLE, G. D. H., *British Working Class Politics, 1832 to 1914*, Routledge & Kegan Paul, 1946.

COLERIDGE, S. T., *On The Constitution of Church and State According to the Idea of Each*, 4th ed., 1852.

COLQUHOUN, J. C., *The System of National Education in Ireland: Its Principle and Practice*, Cheltenham, 1838.

COMBE, G., *Remarks on National Education, Being an Inquiry into the Right and Duty of Government to Educate the People*, Edinburgh, 1847.

CONNELL, W. F., *The Educational Thought and Influence of Matthew Arnold*, Routledge & Kegan Paul, 1950.

CORCORAN, T., *State Policy in Irish Education, A.D. 1536 to 1816*, Fallon, Dublin, 1916.

CORNISH, F. W., *A History of the Church of England in the Nineteenth Century*, 2 vols., Macmillan, 1910.

COSTELLO, N., *John McHale, Archbishop of Tuam*, Dublin, 1939.

COX, J. C. S., *The Life of Cardinal Vaughan*, 2 vols., Herbert & Daniel, 1910.

CRAIK, H., *The State in its Relation to Education*, 1884.

CRUICKSHANK, M., *Church and State in English Education*, Macmillan, 1963.

DALE, A. W. W., *The Life of R. W. Dale of Birmingham*, 2nd ed., 1899.

DALE, R. W., 'Cardinal Manning's Demand on the Rates', *Nineteenth Century*, XIII, January 1883.

DALE, R. W., *History of English Congregationalism*, Hodder & Stoughton, 1907.

DALE, R. W., 'The Cardinal and the Schools: a Rejoinder', *Nineteenth Century*, XIII, March 1883.

DENISON, G. A., *Church Schools and State Interference. A Letter to ... W. E. Gladstone*, 1847.

DENISON, G. A., *Notes of My Life 1805-1878*, 1878.

DENISON, L. E., *Fifty years at East Brent, the Letters of George Anthony Denison 1845-1896*, Murray, 1902.

DENT, H. C., *The Education Act, 1944*, U.L.P., 8th ed., 1960.

DIAMOND, M. G., *The Work of the Catholic Poor School Committee 1847-1905* (unpublished M.Ed. thesis, University of Liverpool), 1963.

DUGDALE, B. E. C., *Arthur James Balfour*, 2 vols., Hutchinson, 1936.

DUNLOP, D., *A Review of the Administration of the Board of National Education in Ireland from its Establishment in 1831 to 1843 with Suggestions for its Improvement*, 1843.

DUNN, D., *National Education, the Question of Questions; Being an Apology for the Bible in the Schools of the Nation*, 2nd ed., 1838.

EAGLESHAM, E., *From School Board to Local Authority*, Routledge & Kegan Paul, 1956.

EAGLESHAM, E., 'Implementing the Education Act of 1902', *British Journal of Educational Studies*, X, 2, May 1962.

EAGLESHAM, E., 'Planning the Education Bill of 1902', *British Journal of Educational Studies*, IX, 1, November 1960.

EDWARDS, J. H., *David Lloyd George*, 2 vols., Sears, New York, 1929.

EVANS, W., and CLARIDGE, W., *James Hirst Hollowell and the Movement for Civic Control in Education*, Northern Counties Education League, Manchester, 1911.

EVENNETT, H. O., 'Catholics and the Universities 1850-1950', in *The English Catholics 1850-1950*, Burns Oates, 1950.

EVENNETT, H. O., *The Catholic Schools of England and Wales*, C.U.P., 1944.

FARRAR, P. N., 'American Influence on the Movement for a National System of Elementary Education in England and Wales, 1830-1870', *British Journal of Educational Studies*, XIV, 1, November 1965.

FISHER, H. A. L., *An Unfinished Autobiography*, O.U.P., 1940.

FITCH, J. G., 'Religion in Primary Schools', *Nineteenth Century*, XXXVI, July 1894.

FITZPATRICK, W. J., *Memoirs of Richard Whately, Archbishop of Dublin*, 2 vols., 1864.

FITZROY, A. W., *Memoirs*, 2 vols., Hutchinson, 6th ed., [193—].

FORSTER, W., 'An Address to Dissenting Sunday School Teachers', in *Tracts of the British Anti-State-Church Association*, 1848.

FRASER, W., *Reasons for the Rejection in Britain of the Irish System*, 1861.

GAINE, M., 'The Development of Official Roman Catholic Educational Policy in England and Wales', in *Religious Education*, Darton, 1968.

GARVIN, J. L., *The Life of Joseph Chamberlain*, 3 vols., Macmillan, 1932-1934.

GLADSTONE, W. E., *Correspondence on Church and Religion*, (ed. Lathbury, D. C.), 2 vols., Murray, 1910.

GLADSTONE, W. E., *The State in its Relations with the Church*, 1838.

GOSDEN, P. H. J. H., 'The Board of Education Act, 1899', *British Journal of Educational Studies*, XI, 1, November 1962.

GOSDEN, P. H. J. H., *The Development of Educational Administration in England and Wales*, Blackwell, Oxford, 1966.

GREEN, J. L., and COLLINGS, J., *The Life of Jesse Collings*, Longmans, 1920.

GREGORY XVI, *Rescript of His Holiness Pope Gregory XVI to the Four Archbishops of Ireland, in reply to the Appeal to the Holy See on the Subject of the National System of Education in Ireland*, Dublin, 1841.

GREGORY, R., *Elementary Education*, National Society's Repository, 1905.

GREGORY, R., 'Religion and the Rates', *Nineteenth Century*, XIII, February 1883.

HALEVY, E., *A History of the English People in the Nineteenth Century*, 6 vols., Benn, 2nd ed., 1949-1952.

HAMILTON, H. H., *The Privy Council and the National Society*, 1850.

HAMMOND, J. L., and B., *Lord Shaftesbury*, Penguin Books, 1939.

HODDER, E., *The Life and Work of the Seventh Earl of Shaftesbury*, 3 vols., 1886-1887.

HOOK, W. F., *On the Means of Rendering More Efficient the Education of the People*, 1846.

HOWARD, C. D. H., 'The Parnell Manifesto of 21 November 1885 and the School Question', *English Historical Review*, 62, 1947.

HUBBARD, J. G., *The Conscience Clause of the Education Department*, 2nd ed., 1865.

HUGHES, D. P., *The Life of Hugh Price Hughes*, 2 vols., Hodder & Stoughton, 1904.

HUGHES, K. M., 'A Political Party and Education; Reflections on the

Liberal Party's Educational Policy 1867-1902', *British Journal of Educational Studies*, VIII, 2, 1960.

INGLIS, K. S., *Churches and the Working Classes in Victorian England*, Routledge & Kegan Paul, 1963.

IREMONGER, F. A., *William Temple, Archbishop of Canterbury ...*, 1948.

JENNINGS, H. C., *The Political Theory of State-Supported Elementary Education in England 1750-1833*, Lancaster Press, Lancaster, Pa., 1928.

JONES, D. K., 'Lancashire, the American Common School, and the Religious Problem in British Education in the Nineteenth Century', *British Journal of Educational Studies*, XV, 3, October 1967.

JUDGES, A. V., 'The Educational Influence of the Webbs', *British Journal of Educational Studies*, X, 1, November 1961.

KAY-SHUTTLEWORTH, J. P., *Four Periods of Public Education ...*, 1862.

KAY-SHUTTLEWORTH, J. P., *Letter to Earl Granville on the Revised Code*, 1861.

KAY-SHUTTLEWORTH, J. P., *Memorandum on the Present State of the Question of Popular Education*, 2nd ed., 1868.

KAY-SHUTTLEWORTH, J. P., *Public Education as Affected by the Minutes of the Committee of the Privy Council from 1846-1852*, 1853.

KEKEWICH, G. W., *The Education Department and After*, Constable, 1920.

KNOX, E. A., *The Tractarian Movement*, 1933.

KNOX, H. M., *Two Hundred and Fifty Years of Scottish Education*, Oliver & Boyd, 1953.

LEESE, J., *Personalities and Power in English Education*, Arnold, 1950.

MACAULAY, T. B., 'Gladstone on Church and State', *Edinburgh Review*, CXXXIX, April 1839.

MᶜCLELLAND, V. A., *Cardinal Manning, His Public Life and Influence 1865-1892*, O.U.P., 1962.

MᶜCLELLAND, V. A., 'The Protestant Alliance and Roman Catholic Schools, 1872-1874', *Victorian Studies*, VIII, 2, December 1964.

MACCOBY, S., *English Radicalism 1786-1832, 1832-52, 1853-86, 1886-1914*, Allen & Unwin, 1935-55.

MACLURE, E., and ALLEN, W. O. B., *Two Hundred Years: the History of the S.P.C.K. 1698-1898*, 1898.

MALTBY, S. E., *Manchester and the Movement for National Elementary Education*, Manchester University Press, 1918.

MANNING, H. E., 'Is the Education Act of 1870 a Just Law?', *Nineteenth Century*, XII, December 1882.

MANNING, H. E., 'Religion and the Rates', *Nineteenth Century*, XIII, February 1883.

MATHEWS, H. F., *Methodism and the Education of the People 1791-1851*, Epworth Press, 1949.

MAURICE, F. (ed.), *The Life of Frederick Denison Maurice*, 2 vols., 1885.

MAURICE, F. D., *Has the Church or the State the Power to Educate the Nation?*, 1839.

MAY, P. R., and JOHNSTON, O. R., 'Parental Attitudes to Religious Education in State Schools', *Durham Research Review*, V, 18, April 1967.

MESCALL, J., *Religion in the Irish System of Education*, Burns Oates, 1957.

MIALL, A., *The Life of Edward Miall*, 1884.

MIALL, E., *The Nonconformist's Sketch Book; a Series of Views of a State-Church and its Attendant Evils*, 1845.

MIALL, E., *The Social Influences of the State-Church*, 1867.

MIALL, E., and TAYLOR, J., *The Church and State Question*, 2nd ed. [1847?].

MOBERLEY, W., and others, *The Churches Survey Their Task*, Report of the Conference ... July 1937 on Church, Community and State, Allen & Unwin, 1937.

MONTMORENCY, J. E. G. DE, *State Intervention in English Education*, C.U.P., 1902.

MONTMORENCY, J. E. G. DE, *The Progress of Education in England*, Knight, 1904.

MOORMAN, J. R. H., *A History of the Church in England*, Black, 1953.

MORLEY, J., *The Life of Richard Cobden*, 2 vols., Macmillan, 1908.

MORLEY, J., *The Life of William Ewart Gladstone*, 3 vols., Macmillan, 1903.

MORLEY, J., *The Struggle for National Education*, 1873.

MURPHY, J., 'Church and State in Education: England and Wales', *The World Year of Education 1966*, Evans, 1966 (1).

MURPHY, J., *The Religious Problem in English Education: The Crucial Experiment*, Liverpool University Press, 1959.

MURPHY, J., 'The Rise of Public Elementary Education in Liverpool', Part 1, 1784-1818; Part 2, 1819-1835; *Transactions of the Historic Society of Lancashire and Cheshire*, Liverpool, 116, 1964; 118, 1966 (2).

MURRAY, R. H., *Studies in the English Social and Political Thinkers of the Nineteenth Century*, Heffer, Cambridge, 1929.

NEWLAND, H., *An Examination of the Scripture Lessons, as Translated and Published by His Majesty's Commissioners of Education in Ireland*, Dublin, 1836.

NORMAN, E. R., *Anti-Catholicism in Victorian England*, Allen & Unwin, 1968.

OVERTON, J. H., *The English Church in the Nineteenth Century*, 1894.

PARKER, C. S., *Life and Letters of Sir James Graham, 1792-1861*, 2 vols., Murray, 1907.

PARKER, C. S. (ed.), *Sir Robert Peel*, 3 vols., 1899.

PEEL, A., *These Hundred Years, a History of the Congregational Union of England and Wales 1831-1931*, Congregational Union, 1931.

PIUS XI, *Divini Illius Magistri* (On the Christian Education of Youth), Catholic Truth Society, 1929.

POWELL, B., *State Education Considered with Reference to Prevalent Misconceptions on Religious Grounds*, 1840.

PUGH, D. R., 'The 1902 Act: the Search for a Compromise', *British Journal of Educational Studies*, XVI, 2, June 1968.

REID, T. W., *The Life of William Edward Forster*, 2 vols., 1888.

RICH, E. E., *The Education Act 1870*, Longmans, 1970.

RICH, R. W., *The Training of Teachers in England and Wales in the Nineteenth Century*, C.U.P., 1933.

RIGG, J. H., *History and Present Position of Primary Education*, 1870.

RIGG, J. H., *National Education*, 1873.

ROBERTSON, J. J., 'The Scottish Solution', *Year Book of Education 1951*, Evans, 1951.

ROGERS, A., 'Churches and Children – A Study in the Controversy over the 1902 Education Act', *British Journal of Educational Studies*, VIII, 1, November 1959.

RUSSELL, LORD J., *Recollections and Suggestions 1813-1873*, 1875.

RUSSELL, LORD J., *Selections from the Speeches of Earl Russell, 1817-1841*, 2 vols., 1870.

SACKS, B., *The Religious Issue in the State Schools of England and Wales 1902-1914*, University of New Mexico Press, Albuquerque, 1961.

SIMON, B., *Studies in the History of Education 1780-1870*, Lawrence & Wishart, 1960.

SIMON, B., *Studies in the History of Education: Education and the Labour Movement 1870-1920*, Lawrence & Wishart, 1965.

SIMON, B. (ed.), *Education in Leicestershire 1540-1940*, Leicester University Press, 1968.

SIMPSON, J., *Necessity of Popular Education as a National Object*, Edinburgh, 1836.

SINCLAIR, J. (ed.), *Correspondence of the National Society with the Lords of the Treasury and with the Committee of Council on Education*, 1839.

SKINNIDER, M., 'Catholic Elementary Education in Glasgow 1818-1918', in Bone, T. R. (ed.), *Studies in the History of Scottish Education 1872-1939*, U.L.P., 1967.

SMITH, F., *The Life and Work of Sir James Kay-Shuttleworth*, Murray, 1923.

SOUTHEY, R., and C. C., *The Life of the Rev. Andrew Bell*, 3 vols., 1844.

SPALDING, T. A., *The Work of the London School Board*, 2nd ed., King, 1900.

SPENCER, A. E. C. W., 'An Evaluation of Roman Catholic Educational Policy in England and Wales 1900-1960', in *Religious Education*, Darton, 1968.

STANLEY, E. G., *Letter of the Rt. Hon. E. G. Stanley, Chief Secretary to His Excellency the Lord Lieutenant Addressed to His Grace the Duke of Leinster*, 1831.

STEPHENS, W. R. W., *The Life and Letters of Walter Farquhar Hook*, 6th ed., 1881.

STRANKS, C. J., *Dean Hook*, Mowbray, 1954.

TAYLOR, A. F., *Birmingham and the Movement for National Education* (unpublished Ph.D. thesis, University of Leicester), 1960.

TAYLOR, G., and SAUNDERS, J. B., *The New Law of Education*, Butterworth, 6th ed., 1965.

THOMPSON, E. P., *The Making of the English Working Class*, Penguin Books, 1968.

TOWNSEND, H., *The Claims of the Free Churches*, Hodder & Stoughton, 1949.

TROPP, A., *The School Teachers*, Heinemann, 1957.

ULLATHORNE, W. B., *Notes on the Education Question*, 1857.

VAUGHAN, H., *Popular Education in England: the Conscience Clause, the Rating Clause, and the Secular Current*, 1868.

VIDLER, A. R., *The Orb and the Cross: A Normative Study in the Relations of Church and State with Reference to Gladstone's Early Writ-*

ings, S.P.C.K., 1945.

VIDLER, A. R., 'The Tractarian Movement, Church Revival and Reform', in *Ideas and Beliefs of the Victorians*, Sylvan Press, 1949.

WEBB, S., *London Education*, Longmans, 1904.

WEST, E. G., 'The Role of Education in Nineteenth Century Doctrines of Political Economy', *British Journal of Educational Studies*, XII, 2, May 1964.

WHATELEY, E. J., *The Life and Correspondence of Richard Whateley, D.D., Late Archbishop of Dublin*, new ed., 1875.

WYSE, W. M., *Notes on Education Reform in Ireland during the First Half of the Nineteenth Century*, Waterford, 1901.

Reports from select committees, commissions and other official sources

(in chronological order)

Reports from the Select Committee appointed to inquire into the education of the lower orders of the metropolis, 1816-18.

Reports from the Select Committee appointed to inquire into the present state of the education of the people in England and Wales, and into the application and effects of the grant made in the last session of parliament for the erection of schoolhouses, and the expediency of further grants in aid of education, 1834, 1835.

Report from the Select Committee appointed to take into consideration the state of the poorer classes in Ireland, 1830.

Annual reports of the Commissioners of Education in Ireland, from 1834.

Report from the Select Committee appointed to examine into the state, funds, and management of the diocesan royal and other schools of public foundation in Ireland, the system of education pursued therein, and how far it may be practicable and expedient to improve and permanently maintain academical education in that country, 1835-36.

Reports by the Lords' Select Committee appointed to inquire into the progress and operation of the plan of education in Ireland, 1837.

Report from the Select Committee on the education of the poorer classes in England and Wales, 1838.

Minutes of the Committee of Council on Education, 1839-58 (continued as Reports of the Committee of Council on Education, 1859-1899).

Correspondence between the Committee of Council on Education and the National Society upon the subject of management clauses; copies of the management clauses as amended; and conditions imposed either upon Roman Catholic schools, or schools of Dissenting Bodies, previously to the advance of any sum of money towards the building of such schools, 1849.

Report from the Select Committee on education in Manchester and Salford, 1852.

Report of the Commissioners appointed to inquire into the state of popular education in England and to consider and report what measures, if any, are required for the extension of sound and cheap elementary education to all classes of people, 1861. (The 'Newcastle Commission'.)

Report of Her Majesty's Commissioners appointed to inquire into the revenues and management of certain colleges and schools ... 1864. (The 'Clarendon Commission'.)

Report from the Select Committee appointed to inquire into the constitution of the Committee of Council on Education, and the system under which the business of the office is conducted; and also into the best mode of extending the benefits of government inspection and the parliamentary grants to schools at present unassisted by the state, 1865-6.

Report of the Commissioners appointed ... to inquire into the education given in schools in England, not comprised within Her Majesty's two recent commissions on popular education and on public schools, 1867-8. (The 'Taunton Commission'.)

Correspondence between the Archbishop of Canterbury and Earl Granville, on the subject of the conscience clause, 1866.

Return of cases in which, between 1861 and 1867 the Education Department has awarded, or entered into correspondence respecting, grants towards building elementary schools ... distinguishing cases in which the Department refused a grant on the ground that children of Dissenters might be excluded from such a school, and stating whether the promoters met it by agreeing to insert a conscience clause ..., 1867.

Return, confined to the municipal boroughs of Birmingham, Leeds, Liverpool and Manchester, of schools for the poorer classes ..., *by J. G. Fitch and D. R. Fearon*, 1870.

Returns of provisions made by each school board in England and Wales, respecting religious teaching and religious observances by children in board schools, stating the cases in which no such provision is made, 1874-79, etc.

Return of the regulations and byelaws at present in force in each school board district in England and Wales respecting the religious teaching ..., 1888.

Reports of the Royal Commission appointed to inquire into the working of the Elementary Education Act, 1886-88. (The 'Cross Commission'.)

Reports of the Board of Education from 1900 (continued as *Reports of the Ministry of Education* and *Reports of the Department of Education and Science*).

Report of the Consultative Committee on the education of the adolescent (Board of Education), 1926.

Report of the Consultative Committee on secondary education ..., (Board of Education), 1938.

Educational Reconstruction (White Paper), 1943.

Statistics of Education 1961 – (Ministry of Education, Department of Education and Science).

Other reports and pamphlets

Archbishops' Committee on Church and State: *Report*, 1917.
Archbishops' Committee on Education: *Report*, 1895.
British and Foreign School Society: *Annual Reports*, from 1811.
British Humanist Association: *NOP survey: moral and religious education, what the people want* (1969).
Catholic Poor School Committee: *Annual Reports*, 1847-1904.
Catholic Education Council: *Annual Reports*, 1905-.
> *The case for Catholic schools*, 2nd ed., 1955.
Census of Great Britain, 1851. Religious worship in England and Wales, abridged from the official report made by H. Mann, 1854.
Central Joint Education Policy Committee: *Christian teaching in schools, a common basis*, 1963.
Central Society of Education: *First Publication*, 1837.
> *Second Publication*, 1838.
Church Information Board: *The church and the schools*, 1954.
Crosby Hall Lectures on Education, 1848.
Fabian Society: *Tract no. 106, The education muddle and the way out*, 1901.
Free Church Federal Council Educational Policy Committee: *Report*, 1959.
Manchester Statistical Society: *Report of a committee ... on the state of education in the Borough of Liverpool 1835-1836*, 1836.
Methodist Education Committee: *Statement of Methodist educational policy adopted by the Methodist Conference ... July 1961*, 1961.
National Education League: *Report of the first general meeting of the National Education League held at Birmingham ... Oct. 1869* (and subsequent annual reports).
National Education Union: *Authorised report of the educational conference held at Leeds ... Dec. 1869*, 1869 (and subsequent annual reports).
National Society: *Annual Reports*, 1812-.
Newman Association: *Reflections on education*, 1968.
Wesleyan Education Committee: *Annual Reports*, 1837-.

Books for further reading

Standard histories of education discuss the relations between church and state in education. Otherwise no one book covers the period dealt with here. A close study of the policies and events leading up to the situation in 1839 will be found in the present writer's *The Religious Problem in English Education: the Crucial Experiment* (1959). Another detailed study is B. Sacks, *The Religious Issue in the State Schools of England and Wales 1902-1914* (1961). The period from 1870 to 1959 has been well surveyed in Majorie Cruickshank, *Church and State in English Education* (1963).

Records of events as seen from the viewpoints of particular groups involved in the controversies described are presented in such accounts as those by Adams, Beales, Beck, Binns, Brown, Burgess, Mathews (listed above); though not impartial, these provide valuable information and often convey much of the atmosphere accompanying the deep differences of opinion recorded. Biographies of leading figures at various periods are extremely helpful, for example, the study of Sir James Kay-Shuttleworth by Frank Smith, A. W. W. Dale's life of his father, and B. M. Allen's biography of Sir Robert Morant; though this last should be read in conjunction with Eric Eaglesham's *The Foundations of Twentieth Century Education* (1967) and other relevant writings by the same author.

A student making a close study of the subject would be well advised to read for himself the more important provisions of the major Acts of Parliament concerned and accounts of the parliamentary debates to which they gave rise, since published summaries are sometimes surprisingly inaccurate and misleading. A great deal of information about the circumstances which led to parliamentary action and on the effectiveness (or ineffectiveness) of earlier legislation will be found in the reports of select committees and royal commissions (especially those of the Newcastle and Cross Commissions), whilst very detailed statistical information, reports of inspectors and alterations in government requirements and regulations can be studied in the annual reports (from 1839) of the Committee of Council and of the administrative bodies which succeeded it. The minutes and reports of some of the voluntary bodies which established schools are normally made available to those engaged in research.

But perhaps the best way in which a student can move outside the framework of knowledge which a preliminary study of the subject will provide will be to study, in relation to some district or region known to him, the reports in local newspapers, the minutes of local school boards and education committees, school log-books and such other sources of local information as are available, to discover the amount, quality and sources of local educational provision, and to learn something of the policies adopted by local churchmen, politicians and others, at least during the major crises referred to in such histories as this. He might also try his hand at examining and describing the attitudes of his own contemporaries, endeavouring to distinguish between declarations of policy based on facts and sincere convictions, and those which are ill founded, tendentious, politically opportunist or merely conventional. This may well inspire in him some sympathy for the historian in his difficult task: it ought certainly to induce that scepticism as to the reliability of the historian's conclusions and generalizations which no student (or writer) of history should ever be without.

Index

Allen, Rev. J., 29
Anglican Church, *see* Church of England
Arnold, M., 81
Ashley, Lord, xiv
and Church of England, 22
and Education Act (1870), 60-1
and Russell's proposals (1839), 20
and 'united education', 25
see also Shaftesbury, Earl of
Authorities Default Act (1904), 95

Baines, E.
and denominational schools, 47
and Voluntaryist movement,
31-2, 37, 47
Balfour, A. J.
and Education Act (1902), 87, 90,
91, 104
Baptists, 3, 91
and state-aid for religious
instruction, 30-1
see also Nonconformists;
Voluntaryists
Beales, A. C. F., 128
Beck, Archbishop (Liverpool), 119,
120
Bell, Dr A., 4, 7, 10
Benson, Archbishop (Canterbury)
and rate-aid for denominational
schools, 78, 79
Bentham, J., 10, 16, 30
Binns, H. B., 5
Birmingham, 4, 42, 50
Education Aid Society, 46, 50
School Board, 70

Birrell, A.
and Education Bill (1906), 97-8,
118
Blomfield, Bishop (London), 17, 20
and status of Established
Church, 23
Booth, C., 7
Bosanquet, B., 83
Bright, Jacob, 60, 68
Bright, John, 43, 49
British and Foreign School Society,
5
and Committee of Council, 29
and finance for schools, 16, 21,
35, 74
and religious instruction, 4-5, 18,
21, 44
and school inspection, 36
and state-aid for education, 10
and teacher-training, 7
political affiliations, 6
Brougham, H., 10, 63
and status of Established
Church, 12, 23-4
educational proposals, 12, 18,
21-2
Bruce, H. A., 47
Butler, R. A.
and Education Act (1944), 111,
113, 114-15, 119, 120

Cambridge University, 2, 17, 38,
46, 106
Catholic Education Council, 104
Catholic Poor School Committee,
36, 61, 78

144

Cecil, Lord H., 87, 90
Central Joint Education Policy
  Committee, 122, 126
Central Nonconformist Committee, 50, 65, 69
Central Society of Education, 18
Chamberlain, J.
  and Education Act (1902), 89-90,
    91
  and Liberal Unionists, 76, 78
  and National Education League,
    50
  and Nonconformists, 65, 76, 78,
    89-90
  and religious instruction, 65, 70,
    76, 77
Charity Commission, 46, 84
Church and state,
  general relations, xiii, xiv, 57,
    62, 110-11, 115, 126, 129
Church Education Society, 39
Church of England
  and 'Concordat' of 1840, 28-30,
    45, 57
  and conscience clause, 38-40, 51,
    56
  and Education Acts, (1870)
    60-1; (1902) 92, 93-4; (1936)
    108-9; (1944) 112, 113, 118,
    119, 128; (1959) 120; (1967)
    124
  and Education Bills, (1896), 82;
    (1906-8), 97, 98, 99
  and educational finance, 17, 34,
    39, 49, 56, 74, 88-9, 104, 120,
    124, 125
  and educational provision, 73,
    88-9, 104, 105, 111, 113-14,
    125
  and Factory Bill (1843), 24
  and Fisher's proposals (1920),
    102, 105
  and 'Irish system', 16, 18-21, 118
  and local control, 42, 108-9
  and Nonconformists, 2, 4, 6, 9,
    23, 54, 121-2, 126, 128
  and parental attitudes, 7-9, 96,
    106, 114
  and political parties, 6, 17, 24,
    74, 87, 96, 97, 98, 114-15
  and privileged status, 1-2, 3-4,
    6, 12, 13, 22, 23, 33, 39, 56
  and rate-aid, 42, 78, 79
  and Reform Bill (1832), 13
  and reforms, 37
  and religious instruction, 5, 6,
    14, 22, 38, 80-1, 87, 106, 113,
    115, 126, 128
  and 'reorganization,' 105-6, 109,
    111
  and Roman Catholics, 62, 97,
    107, 114, 119, 120, 121
  and Russell's proposals (1839),
    19-21
  and school-management, 32-4,
    91-2, 94, 116-17
  and teacher-training, 7, 88, 125
  see also individual Anglicans;
    National Society; Oxford
    movement
Church of England Council for
  Education, 126
Church of Ireland, 15, 49
Church of Scotland
    and Committee of Council, 29
  and education, 11, 12
Clarendon (Public Schools)
  Commission, 46
Clifford, Dr J., 91, 102
Cobden, R.
  and 'religious problem', 18, 43,
    49, 96
Cockerton judgment, 85
Combe, G., 10, 20
Committee of Council on
  Education 26, 27, 47, 49
  administrative burden, 41
  and 'Concordat' of 1840, 28-30
  and conscience clause, 38-40
  and Conservatives, 32
  and denominational schools,
    72
  and Liberals, 32
  and Minutes of 1846, 34-5
  and school boards, 72
  and school inspection, 36
  and school management, 32-3,
    36-7

Com. of Council on Ed.—*cont.*
functions and membership, 21, 22, 41
see also Education Department
'Concordat' of 1840, 28-30, 45, 57
Congregational Union, 73
Congregationalists, 3, 30-1, 37, 73
see also Nonconformists;
Voluntaryists
Conscience clause, 38-40, 44, 50, 56, 57, 63, 93, 115
Conservatives
and Church of England, 6, 17, 24, 74, 87, 96, 98, 114-15
and Committee of Council, 21, 32
and denominational schools, 74, 87, 89
and Education Acts, (1870) 60; (1876) 77; (1891) 77; (1902) 89, 96; (1944) 114-15
and Education Bills, (1896) 82; (1906-8) 98, 99
and Factory Bill (1843), 24
and 'Irish system', 19, 20
and Roman Catholics, 13, 19, 25, 36, 77, 107, 108
and Russell's proposals (1839), 19, 20, 21
and school boards, 62, 71, 77, 81
see also Tories
Controlled schools, 117, 118, 120, 124, 125, 128
Corn Laws, 43
Corporation Act, 13
Councils (county and county borough), 81, 94
and education, 82, 83, 85, 86-7, 91-4, 97-8, 109, 111, 118, 125
Cowper-Temple clause, 58-9, 67, 68, 71, 73
Cross Commission, 63, 68, 69, 71-3, 77, 78, 79, 96-7
Crosskey, Dr H. W., 50
Cumin, P., 68, 72

Dale, Dr R. W., 50, 54, 70, 71, 72, 76

Denison, Bishop (Salisbury), 33
Denison, Rev. G. A., xiv
and conscience clause, 39
and 'management clauses', 33
and status of Established Church, 30
Derby, Earl of, 15
and 'management clauses', 33-4
see also Stanley, E. and Stanley, Lord
Devonshire, Duke of, 84
Disraeli, B., 21
Dissenters, *see* Nonconformists
Dixon, G., 50, 58, 62
Downey, Archbishop (Liverpool), 107

Eaglesham, E., 94
Ecclesiastical Commission, 17
Edinburgh, 37
Education Acts, (1870) 51-63, 65, 71, 85; (1876) 74; (1880) 77; (1891) 77; (1902) 89-95, 115; (1918) 101; (1936) 108, 117; (1939) 108; (1944) 111-19, 125, 127; (1959) 120, 121; (1967) 124
Education and Science, Department of, 124
Education Bills, (1807) 3; (1820) 12; (proposed, 1833) 16; (1847-68) 43, 44, 47; (1896) 82; (1897) 82; 1906-8) 96-100; (1931) 108
Education, Board of, 111, 119
functions, 84, 92
Education Department, 41
and denominational schools, 72, 73
and religious instruction, 63, 66-7, 68-9
and school boards, 72, 73
functions and powers, 41, 62, 74, 84
see also Committee of Council on Education
Education, Ministry of, 124
Education Reform Council, 101
Educational finance, xiii, 10, 11, 12, 15, 16, 17, 21, 34-6, 37, 40-1, 42, 44, 46, 47, 49, 52-6, 72, 73-5,

Educational finance—*cont.*
77, 82, 87, 88-9, 108, 116-17,
125
Educational provision, 5, 10, 11,
18, 37, 41-2, 46, 47, 50, 51-2, 73,
83, 88-9, 103, 104, 105, 111,
113-14, 120, 125, 126
Educational Reconstruction, 111,
112, 113
Endowed Schools Act (1869), 46
Established Church, *see* Church
of England
Evangelical Movement, 3, 17
and Oxford movement, 39

Factory Acts, (1802) 12; (1833) 24;
(1843) 24; (1864) 46; (1867) 46
Fisher, H. A. L.
and denominational authorities,
101-2
and Education Act (1918), 101,
104
Fitch, J. G., 63, 67
Forster, W. E., 47, 49, 54, 84
and Act of 1870, 51-3, 55, 56,
57, 59, 65, 66, 87
Free Church Federal Council,
121-2, 126
Free Church of Scotland, 36
Free Churches, *see*
Nonconformists

Gaine, Rev. M., 128
Gladstone, W. E., 8, 18, 21, 39,
49, 54, 126
and Church of England, 22, 57
and grants for schools, 55-6, 61
and Home Rule, 76, 78
and 'management clauses', 33
and religious instruction, 52,
57-60, 66, 69
Gorst, Sir J., 85, 89
Graham, Sir J., 27
and Factory Bill (1843), 24,
25
Green, T. H., 83
Gregory, Canon R., 67, 77
Gregory XVI, Pope
and 'Irish system', 25

Hadow Report (1926), 105, 106
Hardie, K., 100
Heller, T. E., 63
Holyoake, G. J., 48
Homerton Training College, 37
Hook, Rev. W. F., 8, 30, 43
Howard, Lord, 61
Howley, Archbishop (Canterbury)
and status of Established
Church, 22, 23
Hughes, Rev. H. P., 91
Humanist Association, 127

Independent Labour party, 101
Industrial Schools Act (1866), 46,
78, 81
Inglis, Sir R., 13
Ireland
education in, 3, 11, 15, 24
Home Rule, 76, 78
religion in, 3, 17
Irish Nationalists, 76-7, 78, 89, 91,
107
'Irish system' of education, 15, 118
abandoned, 64
and Archbishop McHale, 24, 64
and National Education League,
51, 64
and Pope Gregory XVI, 25
and Russell's proposals (1839),
19
in Liverpool Corporation
Schools, 18-19, 25, 118

Jews, 2, 9, 36, 96

Kay-Shuttleworth, Sir J., 26, 40,
44, 57
and Minutes of 1846, 37
and Oxford movement, 30, 39
and 'payment by results', 44
educational policies, 26, 27, 47,
48, 84
Kenyon-Slaney, Colonel, 91-2, 94
Kildare Place Society, 11, 15

Labour movement
and religious instruction, 91,
100

Labour movement—*cont.*
  and education, 91
Labour Party
  and Education Act (1967), 123-4
  and Education Bill (1931), 108
  and religious instruction, 100
  and Roman Catholics, 100, 107,
    108
Lancashire Public School
  Association, 43, 49
Lancaster, J., 4
Lansdowne, Marquis of, 20, 22
Leicester School Board, 68
Liberal Unionists, 76, 78, 89
Liberals,
  and Church of England, 13, 17,
    19, 96, 97, 98
  and Committee of Council, 22,
    32
  and Education Acts, (1870)
    51-60, 61-2; (1902) 76, 78, 89,
    91, 96
  and Education Bills, (1906-8)
    96-9
  and Irish Nationalists, 76-7, 89
  and 'Irish system', 18, 19
  and management clauses, 34
  and Minutes of 1846, 37
  and Nonconformists, 19, 49,
    61-2, 96, 99
  and Roman Catholics, 13, 18,
    19, 35-6, 61, 107
  and Russell's proposals (1839),
    19-21
  and school boards, 62, 70
  see also Whigs
Lingen, R. R. W., 40
Liverpool
  Catholic party in, 107
  Corporation Schools, 12, 18-19,
    25, 35, 118
  Education Act (1939), 108, 119
  educational provision in, 4, 5, 52
  School Board, 68
Lloyd George, D., 88, 90
London, 4, 54
  Committee of Friends of
    Voluntary Schools, 44

School Board, 67, 68, 80-1, 82,
    85, 86, 87, 92
Lowe, R., 48

Macaulay, T. B., 37
  on church and state, 23
McHale, Archbishop (Tuam)
  and 'Irish system', 24, 64
McKenna, R.
  Education Bills, (1907) 97;
    (1908) 98
McNeile, Rev. H., 18, 19
Malthus, T. R., 10
Management clauses, 32-4, 35, 36-7,
    91-2, 93, 122
Manchester, 4, 54
  Education Aid Society, 46
  Education Bill Committee, 47
  educational provision in, 52
  School Board, 69, 70
Manchester and Salford Committee
  on Education, 44
Manning, Cardinal H.
  and Education Act (1870), 61,
    67
  and Irish Nationalists, 77
  and rate-aid, 74-5, 78
  and religious instruction, 58,
    71
  and Established Church, 30, 39
Maurice, Rev. F. D., 39
Maynooth College, 3, 11, 22, 36
Melbourne, Lord
  and Nonconformists, 17
  on education, 19
Merthyr Tydfil, 54
Methodists, *see* Wesleyans;
  Nonconformists
Miall, Rev. E.
  and Education Act (1870), 61-2
  and religious census (1851), 37
  and Voluntaryist movement,
    31-2, 45, 47
Mill, J., 10
Mill, J. S., 10
Minutes of 1846, 34-5, 40
Monitorial system, 4, 10, 34
Morant, R., 85
  and Education Act (1902), 86-7,

Morant, R.—*cont.*
89-90, 104
Mundella, A. J., 79

National Council of Evangelical
Free Churches, 80
National Education Association,
79
National Education League, 50, 60,
69, 79
and Nonconformists, 50
and religious instruction, 50, 51,
58, 65, 70
National Education Union, 51, 65,
66
'National' government
and Education Acts, (1936) 108;
(1944) 110-15
National Public School Association,
43, 44
National Society
and 'Concordat' of 1840, 28-30
and conscience clause, 38-40,
51
and educational finance, 16, 21,
35, 87
and Oxford movement, 28, 39
and political parties, 6, 87
and rate-aid, 78, 79
and religious instruction, 5,
22, 38, 87, 106
National Union of Elementary
Teachers, 63
National Union of Teachers, 101
and Education Acts, (1902), 91,
99; (1936) 108
and Education Bill (1908), 99
and religious instruction, 63, 81,
96, 102, 104, 107, 127
Newcastle Commission, 8, 9,
41, 44, 45, 71
Newman, Cardinal J. H., 30, 39
Newman Association, 128
Nonconformists
and Church of England, 2,
4, 6, 9, 23, 54, 121-2, 126, 128
and church rates, 2, 4, 9, 54
and 'Concordat' of 1840, 31
and Education Acts, (1870) 53-4,

61, 65; (1902) 90, 91, 94;
(1936) 108; (1944) 112, 114,
115, 119; (1959) 121-2, 126;
(1967) 124
and educational finance, 17, 49,
75, 88-9
and educational provision, 31,
37, 73, 80, 88-9
and Factory Bill (1843), 24, 30,
31
and Fisher's proposals (1920),
102
and local control, 42-3, 53
and Oxford movement, 30, 50,
80
and political parties, 6, 17,
49, 50, 61, 96
and rate-aid, 42, 53, 54, 80,
94-5
and Reform Bill (1832), 13
and religious census (1851), 37
and religious instruction, 10, 13,
14, 90, 115, 121-2
and Roman Catholics, 35, 65,
76, 77, 107, 119, 120, 121-2
and Russell's proposals (1839),
19, 20, 31
and school boards, 66, 68, 70,
73, 79
and state-aid, 30-1, 37, 49, 115,
121-2
**and teacher-training, 73, 88-9,
99, 125**
and working classes, 7
disabilities, 2, 3, 13, 46, 49
see also individual
Nonconformists; National
Education League; separate
denominations; Voluntaryists
Norfolk, Duke of, 71
Northern Ireland, 129
Nunn, Rev. J., 69

Owen, R., 10
Oxford movement, 17, 30
and Kay-Shuttleworth, 39
and religious instruction, 28, 39
and status of Established
Church, 27-8, 39

Oxford University, 2, 13, 17, 38,
46, 106

Paine, T., 10
Pakington, Sir J., 44
Parents
attitudes to 'religious problem',
6-9, 63, 96, 114, 127-8
'Payment by results', 44-5, 56, 62,
74
Peel, Sir R., 21, 23, 36
and Catholic emancipation, 13
and Committee of Council, 27
and 'religious problem', 24, 27,
36
Pestalozzi, H., 18
Presbyterians, 3, 4
see also Nonconformists;
Voluntaryists
Priestley, J., 10
Protestant Alliance, 67
Protestant Association, 18, 20

Quakers, 2, 3, 4
see also Nonconformists

Radicals, 42
and Education Act (1870), 49,
50, 53, 54, 70
education policies, 6, 13, 16, 18,
43, 62, 81
Ragged Schools, 42
Reform Acts, (1832) 13; (1867) 48,
49
'Religious problem'
defined, 13-14
Ritualists, 42, 92
Roebuck, J. A., 16, 18
Roman Catholics, 3, 4, 67, 71
and Church of England, 62, 97,
107, 114, 119, 120, 121
and comprehensive schools, 124
and conscience clause, 38, 51
and Education Acts, (1870) 61;
(1902) 93-4; (1936) 108;
(1939) 108; (1944) 113, 114,
118-19; (1959) 120; (1967)
124
and Education Bills, (1906-8) 96,

97, 98; (1931) 108
and educational finance, 17,
35, 74, 104, 105, 106, 119-20,
124, 125
and educational provision, 5,
73, 88-9, 103, 104, 111, 114,
120, 125
and Fisher's proposals (1920),
102, 105
and Irish Nationalists, 76-7,
107
and 'Irish system', 19, 24, 64,
118
and local control, 42, 108-9
and Nonconformists, 35, 65, 76,
77, 107, 119, 120, 121-2
and parental attitudes, 7-9, 96,
106, 114, 119
and political parties, 13, 19, 25,
36, 77-8, 100, 107, 108, 124
and rate-aid, 42, 78
and Reform Bill (1832), 13
and religious instruction, 5, 13,
14, 15, 35, 37, 106, 112, 113,
128
and 'reorganization', 105-6, 109,
111
and school inspection, 36
and school management, 36-7,
91-2, 94, 116-17
and 'Scottish solution', 103, 104,
112-13, 118
and teacher-training, 7, 99, 125
and trade unions, 100, 110
see also Catholic Education
Council; Catholic Poor School
Committee; individual
Roman Catholics
Runciman, W.
and Education Bill (1908), 98
Russell, Lord J., 13, 58, 62
and Borough Bill (1853), 44
and proposals of 1839, 19-21,
118
and religious problem, 18, 19
and status of Established
Church, 23

Salisbury, Lord, 69, 87

Salisbury, Lord—*cont.*
  education policy, 77, 78, 89
School boards
  and Denominationalists, 66, 70,
    81
  and educational finance, 53, 54,
    66, 70, 74, 77, 88
  and educational provision, 73-4,
    85, 88
  and local councils, 82, 83, 86-7,
    91, 92
  and Nonconformists, 66, 68,
    70, 73, 79
  and political parties, 62, 63, 70,
    71, 77, 81
  and religious instruction, 57,
    67, 68, 69, 80-1
  control of, 66, 67, 70
  see also individual school boards
Science and Art Department, 84
Scotland
  education in, 11, 16, 20, 103
  religion in, 3, 103-4
  religious instruction in, 64, 103,
    112-13
'Scottish solution', 102-4, 112-13
Secularism, 8, 43, 44, 48, 51, 57,
  58, 61, 70, 91, 100, 127
Select committees on education,
  (1818) 10; (1838) 4, 18
Shaftesbury, Earl of, 61-2
  see also Ashley, Lord
Shaw, G. B., 84
Sheffield School Board, 68
Short, E.
  and religious instruction, 126-7
Simpson, J., 10, 18, 20
Single school areas, 13-14, 38, 40,
  50, 57, 71, 80, 91, 97, 98,
  112, 121, 122
Smith, A., 10
Socialists, 6, 8, 70, 83-4, 91, 100
Special agreement schools, 117
Spencer, A. E. C. W., 128
Spens Report (1938), 105
Stanley, E.
  and 'Irish system', 15, 16, 20
  see also Derby, Earl of
Stanley, E. L., 79

State and church
  general relations, xiii, xiv, 54,
    62, 110-11, 115, 126, 129
Stockport, 4
  School Board, 66
Stowell, Rev. H., 18
Sunday schools, 4, 114
Sutton, Archbishop (Canterbury)
  and Education Bill (1807), 3

Talbot, Bishop (Rochester), 87
Taunton (School Enquiry)
  Commission, 46
Teachers
  and Education Acts, (1870) 63;
    (1902) 91, 99; (1944) 112,
    114, 115, 122
  and Education Bills, (1896) 82;
    (1908) 99
  and 'religious problem', 6-7, 63,
    67, 80-1, 82, 122
  'reserved', 108, 117
  status, 7, 34, 45, 62-3, 80-1
  training, 6, 34, 62-3, 73, 77,
    88-9, 99, 125
  see also National Union of
    Elementary Teachers;
    National Union of Teachers
Temple, Archbishop (Canterbury),
  113
Temple, Bishop (London), 71
Test Acts, 13
The Church Times, 102
The Times
  and 'Irish system', 20
*The Times Educational
  Supplement*, 123
Tories
  and Catholic emancipation, 13
  and Church of England, 6, 17
  and Nonconformists, 17
  see also Conservatives
Tractarians, *see* Oxford movement
Trade unions
  and religious problem, 50, 91,
    100, 101, 110

Ullathorne, Bishop (Birmingham),
  61, 63

Unitarians, 3, 5, 14, 44, 50, 67
    see also Nonconformists

Vaughan, Cardinal H., 43, 51
    and rate-aid, 78
Voluntary aided schools, 116, 124, 125
Voluntaryist movement, 31, 37, 38, 42, 43, 44, 45, 47, 49-50

Wales
    and Education Act (1902), 94
    and school boards, 69
    religion in, 7, 42
Webb, S., 84, 85
Wellington, Duke of, 13
Welsh Educational Alliance
    and religious instruction, 51, 58
Wesleyans, 3, 91
    and Church of England, 6, 122
    and conscience clause, 38, 50
    and educational finance, 17, 35, 74, 88
    and educational provision, 73, 80, 88
    and Factory Bill (1843), 35
    and Oxford movement, 30, 50, 80
    and political parties, 6
    and religious instruction, 14, 50, 65, 127
    and Russell's proposals (1839), 20
    and school inspection, 36
    and school management, 35
    and single-school areas, 50
    and Voluntaryists, 35
    see also Nonconformists;
        National Education League;
        individual Wesleyans
Whately, Archbishop (Dublin), 15
Whigs, 13
    and Church of England, 17
    and Nonconformists, 6, 17
    see also Liberals
Whitbread, S., 3
Wilderspin, S., 6
Woodhouse Moor, 94
Workers' Educational Association, 101
Wyse, T.
    and 'Irish system', 15, 18, 21